The Autobiography of John D. Rockefeller

Random Reminiscences of Man and Events

John D. Rockefeller

PREFACE

Probably in the life of every one there comes a time when he is inclined to go over again the events, great and small, which have made up the incidents of his work and pleasure, and I am tempted to become a garrulous old man, and tell some stories of men and things which have happened in an active life.

In some measure I have been associated with the most interesting people our country has produced, especially in business—men who have helped largely to build up the commerce of the United States, and who have made known its products all over the world. These incidents which come to my mind to speak of seemed vitally important to me when they happened, and they still stand out distinctly in my memory.

Just how far any one is justified in keeping what he regards as his own private affairs from the public, or in defending himself from attacks, is a mooted point. If one talks about one's experiences, there is a natural temptation to charge one with traveling the easy road to egotism; if one keeps silence, the inference of wrong-doing is sometimes even more difficult to meet, as it would then be said that there is no valid defense to be offered.

It has not been my custom to press my affairs forward into public gaze; but I have come to see that if my family and friends want some record of things which might shed light on matters that have been somewhat discussed, it is right that I should yield to their advice, and in this informal way go over again some of the events which have made life interesting to me.

There is still another reason for speaking now: If a tenth of the things that have been said are true, then these dozens of able and faithful men who have been associated with me, many of whom have passed away, must have been guilty of grave faults. For myself, I had decided to say nothing, hoping that after my death the truth would gradually come to the surface and posterity would do strict justice; but while I live and can testify to certain things, it seems fair that I should refer to some points which I hope will help to set forth several much-discussed happenings in a new light. I am convinced that they have not been fully understood.

All these things affect the memories of men who are dead and the lives of men who are living, and it is only reasonable that the public should have some first-hand facts to draw from in making up its final estimate.

When these Reminiscences were begun, there was of course no thought that they should ever go so far as to appear between the covers of a book. They were not prepared with the idea of even an informal autobiography, there was little idea of order or sequence, and no thought whatever of completeness.

It would have been a pleasure as well as a satisfaction to dwell with some fulness upon the stories of daily and intimate companionship which existed for so many years with my close partners and associates, but I realize that while these experiences have always been to me among the great pleasures of my life, a long account of them would not interest the reader, and thus it happens that I have but mentioned the names of only a few of the scores of partners who have been so active in building up the business interests with which I have been associated.

J.D.R.

*March,*1909*.*

4

CONTENTS

Some Old Friends

The Difficult Art of Getting

The Standard Oil Company

Some Experiences in the Oil Business

Other Business Experiences and Business Principles

The Difficult Art of Giving

The Benevolent Trust--The Value of the Cooperative Principle in Giving

CHAPTER I

Some Old Friends

Since these Reminiscences are really what they profess to be, random and informal, I hope I may be pardoned for setting down so many small things.

In looking back over my life, the impressions which come most vividly to my mind are mental pictures of my old associates. In speaking of these friends in this chapter, I would not have it thought that many others, of whom I have not spoken, were less important to me, and I shall hope to refer to this subject of my early friends in a later chapter.

It is not always possible to remember just how one first met an old friend or what one's impressions were, but I shall never forget my first meeting with Mr. John D. Archbold, who is now a vice-president of the Standard Oil Company.

At that time, say thirty-five or forty years ago, I was travelling about the country visiting the point where something was happening, talking with the producers, the refiners, the agents, and actually getting acquainted.

One day there was a gathering of the men somewhere near the oil regions, and when I came to the hotel, which was full of oil men, I saw this name writ large on the register:

John D. Archbold, $4.00 a bbl.

He was a young and enthusiastic fellow, so full of his subject that he added his slogan, "$4.00 a bbl.," after his signature on the register, that no one might misunderstand his convictions. The battle cry of $4.00 a barrel was all the more striking because crude oil was selling then for much less, and this campaign for a higher price certainly did attract attention—it was much top good to be true. But if Mr. Archbold had to admit in the end that crude oil is not worth "$4,00 a bbl.," his enthusiasm, his energy, and his splendid power over men have lasted.

He has always had a well-developed sense of humour, and on one serious occasion, when he was on the witness stand, he was asked by the opposing lawyer:

"Mr. Archbold, are you a director of this company?"

"I am."

"What is your occupation in this company?"

He promptly answered, "To clamor for dividends," which led the learned counsel to start afresh on another line.

I can never cease to wonder at his capacity for hard work. I do not often see him now, for he has great affairs on his hands, while I live like a farmer away from active happenings in business, playing golf, planting trees; and yet I am so busy that no day is long enough.

Speaking of Mr. Archbold leads me to say again that I have received much more credit than I deserve in connection with the Standard Oil Company. It was my good fortune to help to bring together the efficient men who are the controlling forces of the organization and to work hand in hand with them for many years, but it is they who have done the hard tasks.

The great majority of my associations were made so many years ago, that I have reached the age when hardly a month goes by (sometimes I think hardly a week) that I am not called upon to send some message of consolation to a family with whom we have been connected, and who have met with some fresh bereavement. Only recently I counted up the names of the early associates who have passed away. Before I had finished, I found the list numbered some sixty or more. They were faithful and earnest friends; we had worked together through many difficulties, and had gone through many severe trials together. We had discussed and argued and hammered away at questions until we came to agree, and it has always been a happiness to me to feel that we had been frank and aboveboard with each other. Without this, business associates cannot get the best out of their work.

It is not always the easiest of tasks to induce strong, forceful men to agree. It has always been our policy to hear patiently and discuss frankly until the last shred of evidence is on the table, before trying to reach a conclusion and to decide finally upon a course of action. In working with so many partners, the conservative ones are apt to be in the majority, and this is no doubt a desirable thing when the mere momentum of a large concern is certain to carry it forward. The men who have been very successful are correspondingly conservative, since they have much to lose in case of disaster. But fortunately, there are also the aggressive and more daring ones, and they are usually the youngest in the company, perhaps few in number, but impetuous and convincing. They want to accomplish things and to move quickly, and they don't mind any amount of work or responsibility. I remember in particular an experience when the conservative influence met the progressive—shall I say? —or the daring side. At all events, this was the side I represented in this case.

ARGUMENTS VERSUS CAPITAL

One of my partners, who had successfully built up a large and prosperous business, was resisting with all his force a plan that some of us favored, to make some large improvements. The cost of extending the operations of this enterprise was estimated at quite a sum—three million dollars, I think it was. We had talked it over and over again, and with several other associates discussed all the pros and cons; and we had used every argument we could command to show why the plan would not only be profitable, but was indeed necessary to maintain the lead we had. Our old partner was obdurate, he had made up his mind not to yield, and I can see him standing up in his vigorous protest, with his hands in his pockets, his head thrown back, as he shouted "No."

It's a pity to get a man into a place in an argument where he is defending a position instead of considering the evidence. His calm judgment is apt to leave him, and his mind is for the time being closed, and only obstinacy remains. Now these improvements had to be made—as I said before, it was essential. Yet we could not quarrel with our old partner, but a minority of us had made up our minds that we must try to get him to yield, and we resolved to try another line of argument, and said to him:

"You say that we do not need to spend this money?"

"No," he replied, "it will probably prove to be many years before such a sum must be spent. There is no present need for these facilities you want to create, and the works are doing well as they are—let's let well enough alone."

Now our partner was a very wise and experienced man, older and more familiar with the subject than some of us, and all this we admitted to him; but we had made up our minds, as I have said, to carry out this idea if we could possibly get his approval, and we were willing to wait until then. As soon as the argument had calmed down, and when the heat of our discussion had passed, the subject was brought up again. I had thought of a new way to approach it. I said:

"I'll take it, and supply this capital myself. If the expenditure turns out to be profitable the company can repay me; and, if it goes wrong, I'll stand the loss."

That was the argument that touched him. All his reserve disappeared and the matter was settled when he said:

"If that's the way you feel about it, we'll go it together. I guess I can take the risk if you can."

It is always, I presume, a question in every business just how fast it is wise to go, and we went pretty rapidly in those days, building and expanding in all directions. We were being confronted with fresh emergencies constantly. A new oil field would be discovered, tanks for storage had to be built almost overnight, and this was going on when old fields were being exhausted, so we were therefore often under the double strain of losing the facilities in one place where we were fully equipped, and having to build up a plant for storing and transporting in a new field where we were totally unprepared. These are some of the things which make the whole oil trade a perilous one, but we had with us a group of courageous men who recognized the great principle that a business cannot be a great success that does not fully and efficiently accept and take advantage of its opportunities.

How often we discussed those trying questions! Some of us wanted to jump at once into big expenditures, and others to keep to more moderate ones. It was usually a compromise, but one at a time we took these matters up and settled them, never going as fast as the most progressive ones wished, nor quite so carefully as the conservatives desired, but always made the vote unanimous in the end.

THE JOY OF ACHIEVEMENT

The part played by one of my earliest partners, Mr. H.M. Flagler, was always an inspiration to me. He invariably wanted to go ahead and accomplish great projects of all kinds, he was always on the active side of every question, and to his wonderful energy is due much of the rapid progress of the company in the early days.

It was to be expected of such a man that he should fulfil his destiny by working out some great problems at a time when most men want to retire to a comfortable life of ease. This would not appeal to my old friend. He undertook, single handed, the task of building up the East Coast of Florida. He was not satisfied to plan a railroad from St. Augustine to Key West—a distance of more than six hundred miles, which would have been regarded as an undertaking large enough for almost any one man—but in addition he has built a chain of superb hotels to induce tourists to go to this newly developed country. Further than this, he has had them conducted with great skill and success.

This one man, by his own energy and capital, has opened up a vast stretch of country, so that the old inhabitants and the new settlers may have a market for their products. He has given work to thousands of these people; and, to crown all, he has undertaken and nearly completed a remarkable engineering feat in carrying

11

his road on the Florida Keys into the Atlantic Ocean to Key West, the point set out for years ago.

Practically all this has been done after what most men would have considered a full business life, and a man of any other nationality situated as he was would have retired to enjoy the fruits of his labor.

I first knew Mr. Flagler as a young man who consigned produce to Clark & Rockefeller. He was a bright and active young fellow full of vim and push. About the time we went into the oil business Mr. Flagler established himself as a commission merchant in the same building with Mr. Clark, who took over and succeeded the firm of Clark & Rockefeller. A little later he bought out Mr. Clark and combined his trade with his own.

Naturally, I came to see more of him. The business relations which began with the handling of produce he consigned to our old firm grew into a business friendship, because people who lived in a comparatively small place, as Cleveland was then, were thrown together much more often than in such a place as New York. When the oil business was developing and we needed more help, I at once thought of Mr. Flagler as a possible partner, and made him an offer to come with us and give up his commission business. This offers he accepted, and so began that life-long friendship which has never had a moment's interruption. It was a friendship founded on business, which Mr. Flagler used to say was a good deal better than a business founded on friendship, and my experience leads me to agree with him.

For years and years this early partner and I worked shoulder to shoulder; our desks were in the same room. We both lived on Euclid Avenue, a few rods apart. We met and walked to the office together, walked home to luncheon, back again after luncheon, and home again at night. On these walks, when we were away from the office interruptions, we did our thinking, talking, and planning together. Mr. Flagler drew practically all our contracts. He has always had the faculty of being able to clearly express the intent and purpose of a contract so well and accurately that there could be no misunderstanding, and his contracts were fair to both sides. I can remember his saying often that when you go into an arrangement you must measure up the rights and proprieties of both sides with the same yardstick, and this was the way Henry M. Flagler did.

One contract Mr. Flagler was called upon to accept which to my surprise he at once passed with his O.K. and without a question. We had concluded to purchase the land on which one of our refineries was built and which was held on a lease from John Irwin, whom we both knew well. Mr. Irwin drew the contract for the purchase of this land on the back of a large manila envelope that he picked up in the office. The description of the property ran as such contracts usually do until it came to the phrase "the line runs south to a mullen stalk," etc. This seemed to me a trifle indefinite, but Mr. Flagler said:

"It's all right, John. I'll accept that contract, and when the deed comes in, you will see that the mullen stalk will be replaced by a proper stake and the whole document will be accurate and shipshape." Of course it turned out exactly as he said it would. I am almost tempted to say that some lawyers might sit at his feet and learn things about drawing contracts good for them to know, but perhaps our legal friends might think I was partial, so I won't press the point.

Another thing about Mr. Flagler for which I think he deserves great credit was that in the early days he insisted that, when a refinery was to be put up, it should be different from the flimsy shacks which it was then the custom to build. Every one was so afraid that the oil would disappear and that the money expended in buildings would be a loss that the meanest and cheapest buildings were erected for use as refineries. This was the sort of thing Mr. Flagler objected to. While he had to admit that it was possible the oil supply might fail and that the risks of the trade were great, he always believed that if we went into the oil business at all, we should do the work as well as we knew how; that we should have the very best facilities; that everything should be solid and substantial; and that nothing should be left undone to produce the finest results. And he followed his convictions of building as though the trade was going to last, and his courage in acting up to his beliefs laid strong foundations for later years.

There are a number of people still alive who will recall the bright, straightforward young Flagler of those days with satisfaction. At the time when we bought certain refineries at Cleveland he was very active. One day he met an old friend on the street, a German baker, to whom he had sold flour in years gone by. His friend told him that he had gone out of the bakery business and had built a little refinery. This surprised Mr. Flagler, and he didn't like the idea of his friend investing his little fortune in a small plant which he felt sure would not succeed. But at first there seemed nothing to do about it. He had it on his mind for some days. It evidently troubled him. Finally he came to me and said:

"That little baker man knows more about baking than oil refining, but I'd feel better if we invited him to join us—I've got him on my conscience."

I of course agreed. He talked to his friend, who said he would gladly sell if we would send an appraiser to value his plant, which we did, and then there arose an unexpected difficulty. The price at which the plant was to be purchased was satisfactory, but the ex-baker insisted that Mr. Flagler should advise him whether he should take his pay in cash or Standard Oil certificates at par. He told Mr. Flagler that if he took it in cash it would pay all his debts, and he would be glad to have his mind free of many anxieties; but if Mr. Flagler said the certificates were going to pay good dividends, he wanted to get into and keep up with a good thing. It was rather a hard proposition to put up to Mr. Flagler, and at first he declined to advise or express any opinion, but the German stuck to him and wouldn't let him shirk a responsibility which in no way belonged to him. Finally Mr. Flagler suggested that he take half the amount in cash and pay 50 per cent. on account of his debts, and put the other half in certificates, and see what happened. This he did, and as time went on he bought more certificates, and Mr. Flagler never had to apologize for the advice he gave him. I am confident that my old partner gave this affair as much time and thought as he did to any of his own large problems, and the incident may be taken as a measure of the man.

THE VALUE OF FRIENDSHIPS

But these old men's tales can hardly be interesting to the present generation, though perhaps they will not be useless if even tiresome stories make young people realize how, above all other possessions, is the value of a friend in every department of life without any exception whatsoever.

How many different kinds of friends there are! They should all be held close at any cost; for, although some are better than others, perhaps, a friend of whatever kind is important; and this one learns as one grows older. There is the kind that when you need help has a good reason just at the moment, of course, why it is impossible to extend it.

"I can't indorse your note," he says, "because I have an agreement with my partners not to."

"I'd like to oblige you, but I can explain why at the moment," etc., etc.

I do not mean to criticize this sort of friendship; for sometimes it is a matter of temperament; and sometimes the real necessities are such that the friend cannot do as he would like to do. As I look back over my friends, I can remember only a few of this kind and a good many of the more capable sort. One especial friend I had. His name was S.V. Harkness, and from the first of our acquaintance he seemed to have every confidence in me.

One day our oil warehouses and refinery burned to the ground in a few hours—they were absolutely annihilated. Though they were insured for many hundred thousand of dollars, of course, we were apprehensive about collecting such a large amount of insurance, and feared it might take some time to arrange. That plant had to be rebuilt right away, and it was necessary to lay the financial plans. Mr. Harkness was interested with us in the business, and I said to him:

"I may want to call upon you for the use of some money. I don't know that we shall need it, but I thought I'd speak to you in advance about it."

He took in the situation without much explaining on my part. He simply heard what I had to say and he was a man of very few words.

"All right, J.D., I'll give you all I've got." This was all he said, but I went home that night relieved of anxiety. As it turned out, we received the check of the Liverpool, London & Globe Insurance Company for the full amount before the builders required the payments; and while we didn't need his money, I never shall forget the whole-souled way in which he offered it.

And this sort of experience was not, I am grateful to say, rare with me. I was always a great borrower in my early days; the business was active and growing fast, and the banks seemed very willing to loan me the money. About this time, when our great fire had brought up some new conditions, I was studying the situation to see what our cash requirements would be. We were accustomed to prepare for financial emergencies long before we needed the funds.

Another incident occurred at this time which showed again the kind of real friends we had in those days, but I did not hear the full story of it until long years after the event.

There was one bank where we had done a great deal of business, and a friend of mine, Mr. Stillman Witt, who was a rich man, was one of the directors. At a meeting, the question came up as to what the bank would do in case we wanted more money. In order that no one might doubt his own position on the subject, Mr. Witt called for his strong-box, and said:

"Here, gentlemen, these young men are all O.K., and if they want to borrow more money, I want to see this bank advance it without hesitation, and if you want more security, here it is; take what you want."

We were then shipping a large quantity of oil by lake and canal, to save in transportation, and it took additional capital to carry these shipments; and we required to borrow a large amount of money. We had already made extensive loans from another bank, whose president informed me that his board of directors had been making inquiries respecting our large line of discounts, and had stated that they would probably want to talk with me on the subject. I answered that I would be very glad of the opportunity to meet the board, as we would require a great deal more money from the bank. Suffice it to say, we got all we wanted, but I was not asked to call for any further explanations.

But I fear I am telling too much about banks and money and business. I know of nothing more despicable and pathetic than a man who devotes all the waking hours of the day to making money for money's sake. If I were forty years younger, I should like to go into business again, for the association with interesting and quick-minded men was always a great pleasure. But I have no dearth of interests to fill my days, and so long as I live I expect to go on and develop the plans which have been my inspiration for a lifetime.

During all the long period of work, which lasted from the time I was sixteen years old until I retired from active business when I was fifty-five, I must admit that I managed to get a good many vacations of one kind or another, because of the willingness of my most efficient associates to assume the burdens of the business which they were so eminently qualified to conduct.

Of detail work I feel I have done my full share. As I began my business life as a bookkeeper, I learned to have great respect for figures and facts, no matter how small they were. When there was a matter of accounting to be done in connection with any plan with which I was associated in the earlier years, I usually found that I was selected to undertake it. I had a passion for detail which afterward I was forced to strive to modify.

At Pocantico Hills, New York, where I have spent portions of my time for many years in an old house where the fine views invite the soul and where we can live simply and quietly, I have spent many delightful hours, studying the beautiful views, the trees, and fine landscape effects of that very interesting section of the Hudson River, and this happened in the days when I seemed to need every minute for the absorbing demands of business. So I fear after I got well started, I was not what might be called a diligent business man.

This phrase, "diligent in business," reminds me of an old friend of mine in Cleveland who was devoted to his work. I talked to him, and no doubt bored him unspeakably, on my special hobby, which has always been what some people call landscape gardening, but which with me is the art of laying out roads and paths and work of that kind. This friend of thirty-five years ago plainly disapproved of a man in business wasting his time on what he looked upon as mere foolishness.

One superb spring day I suggested to him that he should spend the afternoon with me (a most unusual and reckless suggestion for a business man to make in those days) and see some beautiful paths through the woods on my place which I had been planning and had about completed. I went so far as to tell him that I would give him a real treat.

"I cannot do it, John," he said, "I have an important matter of business on hand this afternoon."

"That may all be," I urged, "but it will give you no such pleasure as you'll get when you see those paths—the big tree on each side and ----"

"Go on, John, with your talk about trees and paths. I tell you I've got an ore ship coming in and our mills are waiting for her." He rubbed his hands with satisfaction—"I'd not miss seeing her come in for all the wood paths in Christendom." He was then getting $120 to $130 a ton for Bessemer steel rails, and if his mill stopped a minute waiting for ore, he felt that he was missing his life's chance.

Perhaps it was this same man who often gazed out into the lake with every nerve stretched to try to see an ore ship approaching. One day one of his friends asked him if he could see the boat.

"No-o, no-o," he reluctantly admitted, "but she's most in sight."

This ore trade was of great and absorbing interest at Cleveland. My old employer was paid $4 a ton for carrying ore from the Marquette regions fifty years ago, and to think of the wickedness of this maker of woodland paths, who in later years was moving the ore in great ships for eighty cents a ton and making a fortune at it.

All this reminds me of my experiences in the ore business, but I shall come to that later. I want to say something about landscape gardening, to which I have devoted a great deal of time for more than thirty years.

THE PLEASURES OF ROAD PLANNING

Like my old friend, others may be surprised at my claim to be an amateur landscape architect in a small way, and my family have been known to employ a great landscape man to make quite sure that I did not ruin the place. The problem was, just where to put the new home at Pocantico Hills, which has recently been built. I thought I had the advantage of knowing every foot of the land, all the old big trees were personal friends of mine, and with the views of any given point I was perfectly familiar—I had studied them hundreds of times; and after this great landscape architect had laid out his plans and had driven his lines of stakes, I asked if I might see what I could do with the job.

In a few days I had worked out a plan so devised that the roads caught just the best views at just the angles where in driving up the hill you came upon impressive outlooks, and at the ending was the final burst of river, hill, cloud, and great sweep of country to crown the whole; and here I fixed my stakes to show where I suggested that the roads should run, and finally the exact place where the house should be.

"Look it all over," I said, "and decide which plan is best." It was a proud moment when this real authority accepted my suggestions as bringing out the most favoured spots for views and agreed upon the site of the house. How many miles of roads I have laid out in my time, I can hardly compute, but I have often kept at it until I was exhausted. While surveying roads, I have run the lines until darkness made it impossible to see the little stakes and flags. It is all very vain of me to tell of these landscape enterprises, but perhaps they will offset the business talks which occupy so much of my story.

My methods of attending to business matters differed from those of most well-conducted merchants of my time and allowed me more freedom. Even after the chief affairs of the Standard Oil Company were moved to New York, I spent most of my summers at our home in Cleveland, and I do still. I would come to New York when my presence seemed necessary, but for the most part I kept in touch with the business through our own telegraph wires, and was left free to attend to many things which interested me—among others, the making of paths, the planting of trees, and the setting out of little forests of seedlings.

Of all the profitable things which develop quickly under the hand, I have thought my young nurseries show the greatest yield. We keep a set of account books for each place, and I was amazed not long ago at the increase in value that a few years make in growing things, when we came to remove some young trees from Westchester County to Lakewood, New Jersey. We plant our young trees, especially evergreens, by the thousand—I think we have put in as many as ten thousand at once, and let them develop, to be used later in some of our planting schemes. If we transfer young trees from Pocantico to our home in Lakewood, we charge one place and credit the other for these trees at the market rate. We are our own best customers, and we make a small fortune out of ourselves by selling to our New Jersey place at $1.50 or $2.00 each, trees which originally cost us only five or ten cents at Pocantico.

In nursery stock, as in other things, the advantage of doing things on a large scale reveals itself. The pleasure and satisfaction of saving and moving large trees—trees, say, from ten to twenty inches in diameter, or even more in some cases—has been for years a source of great interest. We build our movers ourselves, and work with our own men, and it is truly surprising what liberties you can take with trees, if you once learn how to handle these monsters. We have moved trees ninety feet high, and many seventy or eighty feet. And they naturally are by no means young. At one time or another we have tried almost all kinds of trees, including some which the authorities said could not be moved with success. Perhaps the most daring experiments were with horse-chestnuts. We took up large trees, transported them considerable distances, some of them after they were actually in flower, all at a cost of twenty dollars per tree, and lost very few. We were so successful that we became rather reckless, trying experiments out of season, but when we worked on plans we had already tried, our results were remarkably satisfactory.

Taking our experiences in many hundreds of trees of various kinds in and out of season, and including the time when we were learning the art, our total loss has been something less than 10 per cent., probably more nearly 6 or 7 per cent. A whole tree-moving campaign in a single season has been accomplished with a loss of about 3 per cent.

I am willing to admit that in the case of the larger trees the growth has been retarded perhaps two years, but this is a small matter, for people no longer young wish to get the effects they desire at once, and the modern tree-mover does it. We have grouped and arranged clumps of big spruces to fit the purposes we were aiming for, and sometimes have completely covered a hillside with them.

Oaks we have not been successful with except when comparatively young, and we don't try to move oaks and hickories when they have come near to maturity; but we have made some successful experiments with bass wood, and one of these we have moved three times without injury. Birches have generally baffled us, but evergreens, except cedars, have been almost invariably successfully handled.

This planning for good views must have been an early passion with me. I remember when I was hardly more than a boy I wanted to cut away a big tree which I thought interfered with the view from the windows of the dining-room of our home. I was for cutting it down, but some other members of the family objected, though my dear mother, I think, sympathized with me, as she said one day: "You know, my son, we have breakfast at eight o'clock, and I think if the tree were felled some time before we sat down to table, there would probably be no great complaint when the family saw the view which the fallen tree revealed."

So it turned out.

CHAPTER II

The Difficult Art of Getting

To my father I owe a great debt in that he himself trained me to practical ways. He was engaged in different enterprises; he used to tell me about these things, explaining their significance; and he taught me the principles and methods of business. From early boyhood I kept a little book which I remember I called Ledger A— and this little volume is still preserved—containing my receipts and expenditures as well as an account of the small sums that I was taught to give away regularly.

Naturally, people of modest means lead a closer family life than those who have plenty of servants to do everything for them. I count it a blessing that I was of the former class. When I was seven or eight years old I engaged in my first business enterprise with the assistance of my mother. I owned some turkeys, and she presented me with the curds from the milk to feed them. I took care of the birds myself, and sold them all in business-like fashion. My receipts were all profit, as I had nothing to do with the expense account, and my records were kept as carefully as I knew how.

We thoroughly enjoyed this little business affair, and I can still close my eyes, and distinctly see the gentle and dignified birds walking quietly along the brook and through the woods, cautiously stealing the way to their nests. To this day I enjoy the sight of a flock of turkeys, and never miss an opportunity of studying them.

My mother was a good deal of a disciplinarian, and upheld the standard of the family with a birch switch when it showed a tendency to deteriorate. Once, when I was being punished for some unfortunate doings which had taken place in the village school, I felt called upon to explain after the whipping had begun that I was innocent of the charge.

"Never mind," said my mother, "we have started in on this whipping, and it will do for the next time." This attitude was maintained to its final conclusion in many ways. One night, I remember, we boys could not resist the temptation to go skating in the moonlight, notwithstanding the fact that we had been expressly forbidden to skate at night. Almost before we got fairly started we heard a cry for help, and found a neighbour, who had broken through the ice, was in danger of drowning. By pushing a pole to him we succeeded in fishing him out, and restored him safe and sound to his grateful family. As we were not generally expected to save a man's life every time we skated, my brother William and I felt that there were mitigating circumstances connected with this particular disobedience which might be taken into account in the final judgment, but this idea proved to be erroneous.

STARTING AT WORK

Although the plan had been to send me to college, it seemed best at sixteen that I should leave the high school in which I had nearly completed the course and go into a commercial college in Cleveland for a few months. They taught bookkeeping and some of the fundamental principles of commercial transactions. This training, though it lasted only a few months, was very valuable to me. But how to get a job—that was the question. I tramped the streets for days and weeks, asking merchants and storekeepers if they didn't want a boy; but the offer of my services met with little appreciation. No one wanted a boy, and very few showed any overwhelming anxiety to talk with me on the subject. At last one man on the Cleveland docks told me that I might come back after the noonday meal. I was elated; it now seemed that I might get a start.

I was in a fever of anxiety lest I should lose this one opportunity that I had unearthed. When finally at what seemed to me the time, I presented myself to my would-be employer:

"We will give you a chance," he said, but not a word passed between us about pay. This was September 26, 1855. I joyfully went to work. The name of the firm was Hewitt & Tuttle.

In beginning the work I had some advantages. My father's training, as I have said, was practical, the course at the commercial college had taught me the rudiments of business, and I thus had a groundwork to build upon. I was fortunate, also, in working under the supervision of the bookkeeper, who was a fine disciplinarian, and well disposed toward me.

When January, 1856, arrived, Mr. Tuttle presented me with $50 for my three months' work, which was no doubt all that I was worth, and it was entirely satisfactory.

For the next year, with $25 a month, I kept my position, learning the details and clerical work connected with such a business. It was a wholesale produce commission and forwarding concern, my department being particularly the office duties. Just above me was the bookkeeper for the house, and he received $2,000 a year salary in lieu of his share of the profits of the firm of which he was a member. At the end of the first fiscal year when he left I assumed his clerical and bookkeeping work, for which I received the salary of $500.

As I look back upon this term of business apprenticeship, I can see that its influence was vitally important in its relations to what came after.

To begin with, my work was done in the office of the firm itself. I was almost always present when they talked of their affairs, laid out their plans, and decided upon a course of action. I thus had an advantage over other boys of my age, who were quicker and who could figure and write better than I. The firm conducted a business with so many ramifications that this education was quite extensive. They owned dwelling-houses, warehouses, and buildings which were rented for offices and a variety of uses, and I had to collect the rents. They shipped by rail, canal, and lake. There were many different kinds of negotiations and transactions going on, and with all these I was in close touch.

Thus it happened that my duties were vastly more interesting than those of an office-boy in a large house to-day. I thoroughly enjoyed the work. Gradually the auditing of accounts was left in my hands. All the bills were first passed upon by me, and I took this duty very seriously.

One day, I remember, I was in a neighbour's office, when the local plumber presented himself with a bill about a yard long. This neighbour was one of those very busy men. He was connected with what seemed to me an unlimited number of enterprises. He merely glanced at this tiresome bill, turned to the bookkeeper, and said:

"Please pay this bill."

As I was studying the same plumber's bills in great detail, checking every item, if only for a few cents, and finding it to be greatly to the firm's interest to do so, this casual way of conducting affairs did not appeal to me. I had trained myself to the point of view doubtless held by many young men in business to-day, that my check on a bill was the executive act which released my employer's money from the till and was attended with more responsibility than the spending of my own funds. I made up my mind that such business methods could not succeed.

Passing bills, collecting rents, adjusting claims, and work of this kind brought me in association with a great variety of people. I had to learn how to get on with all these different classes, and still keep the relations between them and the house pleasant. One particular kind of negotiation came to me which took all the skill I could master to bring to a successful end.

We would receive, for example, a shipment of marble from Vermont to Cleveland. This involved handling by railroad, canal, and lake boats. The cost of losses or damage had to be somehow fixed between these three different carriers, and it taxed all the ingenuity of a boy of seventeen to work out this problem to the satisfaction of all concerned, including my employers. But I thought the task no hardship, and so far as I can remember I never had any disagreement of moment with any of these transportation interests. This experience in conducting all sorts of transactions at such an impressionable age, with the helping hand of my superiors to fall back upon in an emergency—was highly interesting to me. It was my first step in learning the principle of negotiation, of which I hope to speak later.

The training that comes from working for some one else, to whom we feel a responsibility, I am sure was of great value to me.

I should estimate that the salaries of that time were far less than half of what is paid for equivalent positions to-day. The next year I was offered a salary of $700, but thought I was worth $800. We had not settled the matter by April, and as a favourable opportunity had presented itself for carrying on the same business on my own account, I resigned my position.

In those days, in Cleveland, everyone knew almost everyone else in town. Among the merchants was a young Englishman named M.B. Clark, perhaps ten years older than I, who wanted to establish a business and was in search of a partner. He had $2,000 to contribute to the firm, and wanted a partner who could furnish an equal amount. This seemed a good opportunity for me. I had saved up $700 or $800, but where to get the rest was a problem.

I talked the matter over with my father, who told me that he had always intended to give $1,000 to each of his children when they reached twenty-one. He said that if I wished to receive my share at once, instead of waiting, he would advance it to me and I could pay interest upon the sum until I was twenty-one.

"But, John," he added, "the rate is ten."

At that time, 10 per cent. a year interest was a very common rate for such loans. At the banks the rate might not have been quite so high; but of course the financial institutions could not supply all the demands, so there was much private borrowing at high figures. As I needed this money for the partnership, I gladly accepted my father's offer, and so began business as the junior partner of the new firm, which was called Clark & Rockefeller.

It was a great thing to be my own employer. Mentally I swelled with pride—a partner in a firm with $4,000 capital! Mr. Clark attended to the buying and selling, and I took charge of the finance and the books. We at once began to do a large business, dealing in carload lots and cargoes of produce. Naturally we soon needed more money to take care of the increasing trade. There was nothing to do but to attempt to borrow from a bank. But would the bank lend to us?

THE FIRST LOAN

I went to a bank president whom I knew, and who knew me. I remember perfectly how anxious I was to get that loan and to establish myself favourably with the banker. This gentleman was T.P. Handy, a sweet and gentle old man, well known as a high-grade, beautiful character. For fifty years he was interested in young men. He knew me as a boy in the Cleveland schools. I gave him all the particulars of our business, telling him frankly about our affairs—what we wanted to use the money for, etc., etc. I waited for the verdict with almost trembling eagerness.

"How much do you want?" he said.

"Two thousand dollars."

"All right, Mr. Rockefeller, you can have it," he replied. "Just give me your own warehouse receipts; they're good enough for me."

As I left that bank, my elation can hardly be imagined. I held up my head—think of it, a bank had trusted me for $2,000! I felt that I was now a man of importance in the community.

For long years after the head of this bank was a friend indeed; he loaned me money when I needed it, and I needed it almost all the time, and all the money he had. It was a source of gratification that later I was able to go to him and recommend that he should make a certain investment in Standard Oil stock. He agreed that he would like to do so, but he said that the sum involved was not at the moment available, and so at my suggestion I turned banker for him, and in the end he took out his principal with a very handsome profit. It is a pleasure to testify even at this late date to his great kindness and faith in me.

STICKING TO BUSINESS PRINCIPLES

Mr. Handy trusted me because he believed we would conduct our young business on conservative and proper lines, and I well remember about this time an example of how hard it is sometimes to live up to what one knows is the right business principle. Not long after our concern was started our best customer—that is, the man who made the largest consignments—asked that we should allow him to draw in advance on current shipments before the produce or a bill of lading were actually in hand. We, of course, wished to oblige this important man, but I, as the financial member of the firm, objected, though I feared we should lose his business.

The situation seemed very serious; my partner was impatient with me for refusing to yield, and in this dilemma I decided to go personally to see if I could not induce our customer to relent. I had been unusually fortunate when I came face to face with men in winning their friendship, and my partner's displeasure put me on my mettle. I felt that when I got into touch with this gentleman I could convince him that what he proposed would result in a bad precedent. My reasoning (in my own mind) was logical and convincing. I went to see him, and put forth all the arguments that I had so carefully thought out. But he stormed about, and in the end I had the further humiliation of confessing to my partner that I had failed. I had been able to accomplish absolutely nothing.

Naturally, he was very much disturbed at the possibility of losing our most valued connection, but I insisted and we stuck to our principles and refused to give the shipper the accommodation he had asked. What was our surprise and gratification to find that he continued his relations with us as though nothing had happened, and did not again refer to the matter. I learned afterward that an old country banker, named John Gardener, of Norwalk, O., who had much to do with our consignor, was watching this little matter intently, and I have ever since believed that he originated the suggestion to tempt us to do what we stated we did not do as a test, and his story about our firm stand for what we regarded as sound business principles did us great good.

About this time I began to go out and solicit business—a branch of work I had never before attempted. I undertook to visit every person in our part of the country who was in any way connected with the kind of business that we were engaged in, and went pretty well over the states of Ohio and Indiana. I made up my mind that I could do this best by simply introducing our firm, and not pressing for immediate consignments. I told them that I represented Clark & Rockefeller, commission merchants, and that I had no wish to interfere with any connection that they had at present, but if the opportunity offered we should be glad to serve them, etc., etc.

To our great surprise, business came in upon us so fast that we hardly knew how to take care of it, and in the first year our sales amounted to half a million dollars.

Then, and indeed for many years after, it seemed as though there was no end to the money needed to carry on and develop the business. As our successes began to come, I seldom put my head upon the pillow at night without speaking a few words to myself in this wise:

"Now a little success, soon you will fall down, soon you will be overthrown. Because you have got a start, you think you are quite a merchant; look out, or you will lose your head—go steady." These intimate conversations with myself, I am sure, had a great influence on my life. I was afraid I could not stand my prosperity, and tried to teach myself not to get puffed up with any foolish notions.

My loans from my father were many. Our relations on finances were a source of some anxiety to me, and were not quite so humorous as they seem now as I look back at them. Occasionally he would come to me and say that if I needed money in the business he would be able to loan some, and as I always needed capital I was glad indeed to get it, even at 10 per cent. interest. Just at the moment when I required the money most he was apt to say:

"My son, I find I have got to have that money."

"Of course, you shall have it at once," I would answer, but I knew that he was testing me, and that when I paid him, he would hold the money without its earning anything for a little time, and then offer it back later. I confess that this little discipline should have done me good, and perhaps did, but while I concealed it from him, the truth is I was not particularly pleased with his application of tests to discover if my financial ability was equal to such shocks.

INTEREST AT 10 PER CENT.

These experiences with my father remind me that in the early days there was often much discussion as to what should be paid for the use of money. Many people protested that the rate of 10 per cent. was outrageous, and none but a wicked man would exact such a charge. I was accustomed to argue that money was worth what it would bring—no one would pay 10 per cent., or 5 per cent., or 8 per cent. unless the borrower believed that at this rate it was profitable to employ it. As I was always the borrower at that time, I certainly did not argue for paying more than was necessary.

Among the most persistent and heated discussions I ever had were those with the dear old lady who kept the boarding-house where my brother William and I lived when we were away from home at school. I used to greatly enjoy these talks, for she was an able woman and a good talker, and as she charged us only a dollar a week for board and lodging, and fed us well, I certainly was her friend. This was about the usual price for board in the small towns in those days, where the produce was raised almost entirely on the place.

This estimable lady was violently opposed to loaners obtaining high rates of interest, and we had frequent and earnest arguments on the subject. She knew that I was accustomed to make loans for my father, and she was familiar with the rates secured. But all the arguments in the world did not change the rate, and it came down only when the supply of money grew more plentiful.

I have usually found that important alterations in public opinion in regard to business matters have been of slow growth along the line of proved economic theory—very rarely have improvements in these relationships come about through hastily devised legislation.

One can hardly realize how difficult it was to get capital for active business enterprises at that time. In the country farther west much higher rates were paid, which applied usually to personal loans on which a business risk was run, but it shows how different the conditions for young business men were then than now.

A NIMBLE BORROWER

Speaking of borrowing at the banks reminds me of one of the most strenuous financial efforts I ever made. We had to raise the money to accept an offer for a large business. It required many hundreds of thousands of dollars—and in cash—securities would not answer. I received the message at about noon and had to get off on the three-o'clock train. I drove from bank to bank, asking each president or cashier, whomever I could find first, to get ready for me all the funds he could possibly lay hands on. I told them I would be back to get the money later. I rounded up all of our banks in the city, and made a second journey to get the money, and kept going until I secured the necessary amount. With this I was off on the three-o'clock train, and closed the transaction. In these early days I was a good deal of a traveler, visiting our plants, making new connections, seeing people, arranging plans to extend our business—and it often called for very rapid work.

RAISING CHURCH FUNDS

When I was but seventeen or eighteen, I was elected as a trustee in the church. It was a mission branch, and occasionally I had to hear members who belonged to the main body speak of the mission as though it were not quite so good as the big mother church. This strengthened our resolve to show them that we could paddle our own canoe.

Our first church was not a very grand affair, and there was a mortgage of $2,000 on it which had been a dispiriting influence for years.

The holder of the mortgage had long demanded that he should be paid, but somehow even the interest was barely kept up, and the creditor finally threatened to sell us out. As it happened, the money had been lent by a deacon in the church, but notwithstanding this fact, he felt that he should have his money, and perhaps he really needed it. Anyhow, he proposed to take such steps as were necessary to get it. The matter came to a head one Sunday morning, when the minister announced from the pulpit that the $2,000 would have to be raised, or we should lose our church building. I therefore found myself at the door of the church as the congregation came and went.

As each member came by, I buttonholed him, and got him to promise to give something toward the extinguishing of that debt. I pleaded and urged, and almost threatened. As each one promised, I put his name and the amount down in my little book, and continued to solicit from every possible subscriber.

This campaign for raising the money which started that morning after church, lasted for several months. It was a great undertaking to raise such a sum of money in small amounts ranging from a few cents to the more magnificent promises of gifts to be paid at the rate of twenty-five or fifty cents per week. The plan absorbed me. I contributed what I could, and my first ambition to earn more money was aroused by this and similar undertakings in which I was constantly engaged.

But at last, the $2,000 was all in hand and a proud day it was when the debt was extinguished. I hope the members of the mother church were properly humiliated to see how far we had gone beyond their expectations, but I do not now recall that they expressed the surprise that we flattered ourselves they must have felt.

The begging experiences I had at that time were full of interest. I went at the task with pride rather than the reverse, and I continued it until my increasing cares and responsibilities compelled me to resign the actual working out of details to others.

CHAPTER III

The Standard Oil Company

It would be surprising if in an organization which included a great number of men there should not be an occasional employee here and there who acted, in connection with the business or perhaps in conducting his own affairs, in a way which might be criticized. Even in a comparatively small organization it is well-nigh impossible to restrain this occasional man who is over-zealous for his own or his company's advancement. To judge the character of all the members of a great organization or the organization itself by the actions of a few individuals would be manifestly unfair.

It has been said that I forced the men who became my partners in the oil business to join with me. I would not have been so short-sighted. If it were true that I followed such tactics, I ask, would it have been possible to make of such men life-long companions? Would they accept, and remain for many years in positions of the greatest trust, and finally, could anyone have formed of such men, if they had been so browbeaten, a group which has for all these years worked in loyal harmony, with fair dealing among themselves as well as with others, building up efficiency and acting in entire unity? This powerful organization has not only lasted but its efficiency has increased. For fourteen years I have been out of business, and in eight or ten years went only once to the company's office.

In the summer of 1907, I visited again the room at the top of the Standard Oil Company's building, where the officers of the company and the heads of departments have had their luncheon served for many years. I was surprised to find so many men who had come to the front since my last visit years ago. Afterward I had an opportunity to talk with old associates and many new ones, and it was a source of great gratification to me to find that the same spirit of cooperation and harmony existed unchanged. This practice of lunching together, a hundred or more at long tables in most intimate and friendly association, is another indication of what I contend, slight as it may seem to be at first thought. Would these people seek each other's companionship day after day if they had been forced into this relation? People in such a position do not go on for long in a pleasant and congenial intimacy.

For years the Standard Oil Company has developed step by step, and I am convinced that it has done well its work of supplying to the people the products from petroleum at prices which have decreased as the efficiency of the business has been built up. It gradually extended its services first to the large centers, and then to towns, and now to the smallest places, going to the homes of its customers, delivering the oil to suit the convenience of the actual users. This same system is being followed out in various parts of the world. The company has, for example, three thousand tank wagons supplying American oil to towns and even small hamlets in Europe. Its own depots and employees deliver it in a somewhat similar way in Japan, China, India, and the chief countries of the world. Do you think this trade has been developed by anything but hard work?

This plan of selling our products direct to the consumer and the exceptionally rapid growth of the business bred a certain antagonism which I suppose could not have been avoided, but this same idea of dealing with the consumer directly has been followed by others and in many lines of trade, without creating, so far as I recall, any serious opposition.

This is a very interesting and important point, and I have often wondered if the criticism which centered upon us did not come from the fact that we were among the first, if not the first, to work out the problems of direct selling to the user on a broad scale. This was done in a fair spirit and with due consideration for every one's rights. We did not ruthlessly go after the trade of our competitors and attempt to ruin it by cutting prices or instituting a spy system. We had set ourselves the task of building up as rapidly and as broadly as possible the volume of consumption. Let me try to explain just what happened.

To get the advantage of the facilities we had in manufacture, we sought the utmost market in all lands—we needed volume. To do this we had to create selling methods far in advance of what then existed; we had to dispose of two, or three, or four gallons of oil where one had been sold before, and we could not rely upon the usual trade channels then existing to accomplish this. It was never our purpose to interfere with a dealer who adequately cultivated his field of operations, but when we saw a new opportunity or a new place for extending the sale by further and effective facilities, we made it our business to provide them. In this way we opened many new lines in which others have shared. In this development we had to employ many comparatively new men. The ideal way to supply material for higher positions is, of course, to recruit the men from among the youngest in the company's service, but our expansion was too rapid to permit this in all cases. That some of these employees were over-zealous in going after sales it would not be surprising to learn, but they were acting in violation of the expressed and known wishes of the company. But even these instances, I am convinced, occurred so seldom, by comparison with the number of transactions we carried on, that they were really the exceptions that proved the rule.

Every week in the year for many, many years, this concern has brought into this country more than a million dollars gold, all from the products produced by American labor. I am proud of the record, and believe most Americans will be when they understand some things better. These achievements, the development of this great foreign trade, the owning of ships to carry the oil in bulk by the most economical methods, the sending out of men to fight for the world's markets, have cost huge sums of money, and the vast capital employed could not be raised nor controlled except by such an organization as the Standard is to-day.

To give a true picture of the early conditions, one must realize that the oil industry was considered a most hazardous undertaking, not altogether unlike the speculative mining undertakings we hear so much of to-day. I well remember my old and distinguished friend, Rev. Thomas W. Armitage, for some forty years pastor of a great New York church, warning me that it was worse than folly to extend our plants and our operations. He was sure we were running unwarranted risks, that our oil supply would probably fail, the demand would decline, and he, with many others, sometimes I thought almost everybody, prophesied ruin.

None of us ever dreamed of the magnitude of what proved to be the later expansion. We did our day's work as we met it, looking forward to what we could see in the distance and keeping well up to our opportunities, but laying our foundations firmly. As I have said, capital was most difficult to secure, and it was not easy to interest conservative men in this adventurous business. Men of property were afraid of it, though in rare cases capitalists were induced to unite with us to a limited extent. If they bought our stock at all, they took a little of it now and then as an experiment, and we were painfully conscious that they often declined to buy new stock with many beautiful expressions of appreciation.

The enterprise being so new and novel, on account of the fearfulness of certain holders in reference to its success, we frequently had to take stock to keep it from going begging, but we had such confidence in the fundamental value of the concern that we were willing to assume this risk. There are always a few men in an undertaking of this kind who would risk all on their judgment of the final result, and if the enterprise had failed, these would have been classed as visionary adventurers, and perhaps with good reason.

The 60,000 men who are at work constantly in the service of the company are kept busy year in and year out. The past year has been a time of great contraction, but the Standard has gone on with its plans unchecked, and the new works and buildings have not been delayed on account of lack of capital or fear of bad times. It pays its workmen well, it cares for them when sick, and pensions them when old. It has never had any important strikes, and if there is any better function of business management than giving profitable work to employees year after year, in good times and bad, I don't know what it is.

Another thing to be remembered about this so-called "octopus" is that there has been no "water" introduced into its capital (perhaps we felt that oil and water would not have mixed); nor in all these years has any one had to wait for money which the Standard owed. It has suffered from great fires and losses, but it has taken care of its affairs in such a way that it has not found it necessary to appeal to the general public to place blocks of bonds or stock; it has used no underwriting syndicates or stock-selling schemes in any form, and it has always managed to finance new oil field operations when called upon.

It is a common thing to hear people say that this company has crushed out its competitors. Only the uninformed could make such an assertion. It has and always has had, and always will have,

42

hundreds of active competitors; it has lived only because it has managed its affairs well and economically and with great vigor. To speak of competition for a minute: Consider not only the able people who compete in refining oil, but all the competition in the various trades which make and sell by-products—a great variety of different businesses. And perhaps of even more importance is the competition in foreign lands. The Standard is always fighting to sell the American product against the oil produced from the great fields of Russia, which struggles for the trade of Europe, and the Burma oil, which largely affects the market in India. In all these various countries we are met with tariffs which are raised against us, local prejudices, and strange customs. In many countries we had to teach the people—the Chinese, for example— to burn oil by making lamps for them; we packed the oil to be carried by camels or on the backs of runners in the most remote portions of the world; we adapted the trade to the needs of strange folk. Every time we succeeded in a foreign land, it meant dollars brought to this country, and every time we failed, it was a loss to our nation and its workmen.

One of our greatest helpers has been the State Department in Washington. Our ambassadors and ministers and consuls have aided to push our way into new markets to the utmost corners of the world.

I think I can speak thus frankly and enthusiastically because the working out of many of these great plans has developed largely since I retired from the business fourteen years ago.

The Standard has not now, and never did have a royal road to supremacy, nor is its success due to any one man, but to the multitude of able men who are working together. If the present managers of the company were to relax efforts, allow the quality of their product to degenerate, or treat their customers badly, how long would their business last? About as long as any other neglected business. To read some of the accounts of the affairs of the company, one would think that it had such a hold on the oil trade that the directors did little but come together and declare dividends. It is a pleasure for me to take this opportunity to pay tribute to the work these men are doing, not only for the company they serve, but for the foreign trade of our country; for more than half of all the product that the company makes is sold outside of the United States. If, in place of these directors, the business were taken over and run by anyone but experts, I would sell my interest for any price I could get. To succeed in a business requires the best and most earnest men to manage it, and the best men rise to the top. Of its origin and early plans I will speak later.

THE MODERN CORPORATION

Beyond question there is a suspicion of corporations. There may be reason for such suspicion very often; for a corporation may be moral or immoral, just as a man may be moral or the reverse; but it is folly to condemn all corporations because some are bad, or even to be unduly suspicious of all, because some are bad. But the corporation in form and character has come to stay—that is a thing that may be depended upon. Even small firms are becoming corporations, because it is a convenient form of partnership.

It is equally true that combinations of capital are bound to continue and to grow, and this need not alarm even the most timid if the corporation, or the series of corporations, is properly conducted with due regard for the rights of others. The day of individual competition in large affairs is past and gone—you might just as well argue that we should go back to hand labor and throw away our efficient machines—and the sober good sense of the people will accept this fact when they have studied and tried it out. Just see how the list of stockholders in the great corporations is increasing by leaps and bounds. This means that all these people are becoming partners in great businesses. It is a good thing—it will bring a feeling of increased responsibility to the managers of the corporations and will make the people who have their interests involved study the facts impartially before condemning or attacking them.

On this subject of industrial combinations, I have often expressed my opinions; and, as I have not changed my mind, I am not averse to repeating them now, especially as the subject seems again to be so much in the public eye.

The chief advantages from industrial combinations are those which can be derived from a cooperation of persons and aggregation of capital. Much that one man cannot do alone two can do together, and once admit the fact that cooperation, or, what is the same thing, combination, is necessary on a small scale, the limit depends solely upon the necessities of business. Two persons in partnership may be a sufficiently large combination for a small business, but if the business grows or can be made to grow, more persons and more capital must be taken in. The business may grow so large that a partnership ceases to be a proper instrumentality for its purposes, and then a corporation becomes a necessity. In most countries, as in England, this form of industrial combination is sufficient for a business co-extensive with the parent country, but it is not so in America. Our federal form of government making every corporation created by a state foreign to every other state, renders it necessary for persons doing business through corporate agency to organize corporations in some or many of the different states in which their business is located. Instead of doing business through the agency of one

45

corporation they must do business through the agencies of several corporations. If the business is extended to foreign countries, and Americans are not to-day satisfied with home markets alone, it will be found helpful and possibly necessary to organize corporations in such countries, for Europeans are prejudiced against foreign corporations, as are the people of many of our states. These different corporations thus become cooperation agencies in the same business and are held together by common ownership of their stocks.

It is too late to argue about advantages of industrial combinations. They are a necessity. And if Americans are to have the privilege of extending their business in all the states of the Union, and into foreign countries as well, they are a necessity on a large scale, and require the agency of more than one corporation.

The dangers are that the power conferred by combination may be abused, that combinations may be formed for speculation in stocks rather than for conducting business, and that for this purpose prices may be temporarily raised instead of being lowered. These abuses are possible to a greater or less extent in all combinations, large or small, but this fact is no more of an argument against combinations than the fact that steam may explode is an argument against steam. Steam is necessary and can be made comparatively safe. Combination is necessary and its abuses can be minimized; otherwise, our legislators must acknowledge their incapacity to deal with the most important instrument of industry.

In the hearing of the Industrial Commission in 1899, I then said that if I were to suggest any legislation regarding industrial combinations it would be: First, Federal legislation under which corporations may be created and regulated, if that be possible. Second, in lieu thereof, state legislation as nearly uniform as possible, encouraging combinations of persons and capital for the purpose of carrying on industries, but permitting state supervision, not of a character to hamper industries, but sufficient to prevent frauds upon the public. I still feel as I did in 1899.

THE NEW OPPORTUNITIES

I am far from believing that this will adversely affect the individual. The great economic era we are entering will give splendid opportunity to the young man of the future. One often hears the men of this new generation say that they do not have the chances that their fathers and grandfathers had. How little they know of the disadvantages from which we suffered! In my young manhood we had everything to do and nothing to do it with; we had to hew our own paths along new lines; we had little experience to go on. Capital was most difficult to get, credits were mysterious things. Whereas now we have a system of commercial ratings, everything was then haphazard and we suffered from a stupendous war and all the disasters which followed.

Compare this day with that. Our comforts and opportunities are multiplied a thousand-fold. The resources of our great land are now actually opening up and are scarcely touched; our home markets are vast, and we have just begun to think of the foreign peoples we can serve—the people who are years behind us in civilization. In the East a quarter of the human race is just awakening. The men of this generation are entering into a heritage which makes their fathers' lives look poverty-stricken by comparison. I am naturally an optimist, and when it comes to a statement of what our people will accomplish in the future, I am unable to express myself with sufficient enthusiasm.

There are many things we must do to attain the highest benefit from all these great blessings; and not the least of these is to build up our reputation throughout the whole world.

The great business interests will, I hope, so comport themselves that foreign capital will consider it a desirable thing to hold shares in American companies. It is for Americans to see that foreign investors are well and honestly treated, so that they will never regret purchases of our securities.

I may speak thus frankly, because I am an investor in many American enterprises, but a controller of none (with one exception, and that a company which has not been much of a dividend payer), and I, like all the rest, am dependent upon the honest and capable administration of the industries. I firmly and sincerely believe that they will be so managed.

THE AMERICAN BUSINESS MAN

You hear a good many people of pessimistic disposition say much about greed in American life. One would think to hear them talk that we were a race of misers in this country. To lay too much stress upon the reports of greed in the newspapers would be folly, since their function is to report the unusual and even the abnormal. When a man goes properly about his daily affairs, the public prints say nothing; it is only when something extraordinary happens to him that he is discussed. But because he is thus brought into prominence occasionally, you surely would not say that these occasions represented his normal life. It is by no means for money alone that these active-minded men labor—they are engaged in a fascinating occupation. The zest of the work is maintained by something better than the mere accumulation of money, and, as I think I have said elsewhere, the standards of business are high and are getting better all the time.

I confess I have no sympathy with the idea so often advanced that our basis of all judgments in this country is founded on money. If this were true, we should be a nation of money hoarders instead of spenders. Nor do I admit that we are so small-minded a people as to be jealous of the success of others. It is the other way about: we are the most extraordinarily ambitious, and the success of one man in any walk of life spurs the others on. It does not sour them, and it is a libel even to suggest so great a meanness of spirit.

In reading the newspapers, where so much is taken for granted in considering things on a money standard, I think we need some of the sense of humor possessed by an Irish neighbor of mine, who built what we regarded as an extremely ugly house, which stood out in bright colors as we looked from our windows. My taste in architecture differed so widely from that affected by my Irish friend, that we planted out the view of his house by moving some large trees to the end of our property. Another neighbor who watched this work going on asked Mr. Foley why Mr. Rockefeller moved all these big trees and cut off the view between the houses. Foley, with the quick wit of his country, responded instantly: "It's envy, they can't stand looking at the evidence of me prosperity."

In my early days men acted just as they do now, no doubt. When there was anything to be done for general trade betterment, almost every man had some good reason for believing that his case was a special one different from all the rest. For every foolish thing he did, or wanted to do, for every business-like plan he had, he always pleaded that it was necessary in his case. He was the one man who had to sell at less than cost, to disrupt all the business plans of others in his trade, because his individual position was so absolutely different from all the rest. It was often a heart-breaking undertaking to convince those men that the perfect occasion which would lead to the perfect opportunity would never come, even if they waited until the crack o' doom.

Then, again, we had the type of man who really never knew all the facts about his own affairs. Many of the brightest kept their books in such a way that they did not actually know when they were making money on a certain operation and when they were losing. This unintelligent competition was a hard matter to contend with. Good old-fashioned common sense has always been a mighty rare commodity. When a man's affairs are not going well, he hates to study the books and face the truth. From the first, the men who managed the Standard Oil Company kept their books intelligently as well as correctly. We knew how much we made and where we gained or lost. At least, we tried not to deceive ourselves.

My ideas of business are no doubt old-fashioned, but the fundamental principles do not change from generation to generation, and sometimes I think that our quick-witted American business men, whose spirit and energy are so splendid, do not always sufficiently study the real underlying foundations of business management. I have spoken of the necessity of being frank and honest with oneself about one's own affairs: many people assume that they can get away from the truth by avoiding thinking about it, but the natural law is inevitable, and the sooner it is recognized, the better.

One hears a great deal about wages and why they must be maintained at a high level, by the railroads, for example. A laborer is worthy of his hire, no less, but no more, and in the long run he must contribute an equivalent for what he is paid. If he does not do this, he is probably pauperized, and you at once throw out the balance of things. You can't hold up conditions artificially, and you can't change the underlying laws of trade. If you try, you must inevitably fail. All this may be trite and obvious, but it is remarkable how many men overlook what should be the obvious. These are facts we can't get away from—a business man must adapt himself to the natural conditions as they exist from month to month and year to year. Sometimes I feel that we Americans think we can find a short road to success, and it may appear that often this feat is accomplished; but real efficiency in work comes from knowing your facts and building upon that sure foundation.

Many men of wealth do not retire from business even when they can. They are not willing to be idle, or they have a just pride in their work and want to perfect the plans in which they have faith, or, what is of still more consequence, they may feel the call to expand and build up for the benefit of their employees and associates, and these men are the great builders up in our country. Consider for a moment how much would have been left undone if our prosperous American business men had sat down with folded hands when they had acquired a competency. I have respect for all these reasons, but if a man has succeeded, he has brought upon himself corresponding responsibilities, and our institutions devoted to helping men to help themselves need the brain of the American business man as well as part of his money.

Some of these men, however, are so absorbed in their business affairs that they hardly have time to think of anything else. If they do interest themselves in a work outside of their own office and undertake to raise money, they begin with an apology, as if they are ashamed of themselves.

"I am no beggar," I have heard many of them say, to which I could only reply: "I am sorry you feel that way about it."

I have been this sort of beggar all my life and the experiences I have had were so interesting and important to me that I will venture to speak of them in a later chapter.

CHAPTER IV

Some Experiences in the Oil Business

During the years when I was just coming to man's estate, the produce business of Clark & Rockefeller went on prosperously, and in the early sixties we organized a firm to refine and deal in oil. It was composed of Messrs. James and Richard Clark, Mr. Samuel Andrews, and the firm of Clark & Rockefeller, who were the company. It was my first direct connection with the oil trade. As the new concern grew the firm of Clark & Rockefeller was called upon to supply a large special capital. Mr. Samuel Andrews was the manufacturing man of the concern, and he had learned the process of cleansing the crude oil by the use of sulphury acid.

In 1865 the partnership was dissolved; it was decided that the cash assets should be collected and the debts paid, but this left the plant and the good-will to be disposed of. It was suggested that they should go to the highest bidder among ourselves. This seemed a just settlement to me, and the question came up as to when the sale should be held and who would conduct it. My partners had a lawyer in the room to represent them, though I had not considered having a legal representative; I thought I could take care of so simple a transaction. The lawyer acted as the auctioneer, and it was suggested that we should go on with the sale then and there. All agreed, and so the auction began.

I had made up my mind that I wanted to go into the oil trade, not as a special partner, but actively on a larger scale, and with Mr. Andrews wished to buy that business. I thought that I saw great opportunities in refining oil, and did not realize at that time that the whole oil industry would soon be swamped by so many men rushing into it. But I was full of hope, and I had already arranged to get financial accommodation to an amount that I supposed would easily pay for the plant and good-will. I was willing to give up the other firm of Clark & Rockefeller, and readily settled that later—my old partner, Mr. Clark, taking over the business.

The bidding began, I think, at $500 premium. I bid a thousand; they bid two thousand; and so on, little by little, the price went up. Neither side was willing to stop bidding, and the amount gradually rose until it reached $50,000, which was much more than we supposed the concern to be worth. Finally, it advanced to $60,000, and by slow stages to $70,000, and I almost feared for my ability to buy the business and have the money to pay for it. At last the other side bid $72,000. Without hesitation I said $72,500. Mr. Clark then said:

"I'll go no higher, John; the business is yours."

"Shall I give you a check for it now?" I suggested.

"No," Mr. Clark said, "I'm glad to trust you for it; settle at your convenience."

The firm of Rockefeller & Andrews was then established, and this was really my start in the oil trade. It was my most important business for about forty years until, at the age of about fifty-six, I retired.

The story of the early history of the oil trade is too well known to bear repeating in detail. The cleansing of crude petroleum was a simple and easy process, and at first the profits were very large. Naturally, all sorts of people went into it: the butcher, the baker, and the candlestick-maker began to refine oil, and it was only a short time before more of the finished product was put on the market than could possibly be consumed. The price went down and down until the trade was threatened with ruin. It seemed absolutely necessary to extend the market for oil by exporting to foreign countries, which required a long and most difficult development; and also to greatly improve the processes of refining so that oil could be made and sold cheaply, yet with a profit, and to use as by-products all of the materials which in the less-efficient plants were lost or thrown away.

These were the problems which confronted us almost at the outset, and this great depression led to consultations with our neighbors and friends in the business in the effort to bring some order out of what was rapidly becoming a state of chaos. To accomplish all these tasks of enlarging the market and improving the methods of manufacture in a large way was beyond the power or ability of any concern as then constituted. It could only be done, we reasoned, by increasing our capital and availing ourselves of the best talent and experience.

It was with this idea that we proceeded to buy the largest and best refining concerns and centralize the administration of them with a view to securing greater economy and efficiency. The business grew faster than we had anticipated.

This enterprise, conducted by men of application and ability working hard together, soon built up unusual facilities in manufacture, in transportation, in finance, and in extending markets. We had our troubles and set-backs; we suffered from some severe fires; and the supply of crude oil was most uncertain. Our plans were constantly changed by changed conditions. We developed great facilities in an oil centre, erected storage tanks, and connected pipe-lines; then the oil failed and our work was thrown away. At best it was a speculative trade, and I wonder that we managed to pull through so often; but we were gradually learning how to conduct a most difficult business.

FOREIGN MARKETS

Several years ago, when asked how our business grew to such large proportions I explained that our first organization was a partnership and afterward a corporation in Ohio. That was sufficient for a local refining business. But, had we been dependent solely upon local business, we should have failed long since. We were forced to extend our markets into every part of the world. This made the sea-board cities a necessary place of business, and we soon discovered that manufacturing for export could be more economically carried on there; hence refineries were established at Brooklyn, at Bayonne, at Philadelphia, at Baltimore, and necessary corporations were organized in the different states.

We soon discovered, as the business grew, that the primary method of transporting oil in barrels could not last. The package often cost more than the contents, and the forests of the country were not sufficient to supply cheaply the necessary material for an extended time. Hence we devoted attention to other methods of transportation, adopted the pipe-line system, and found capital for pipe-line construction equal to the necessities of the business.

To operate pipe-lines required franchises from the states in which they were located—and consequently corporations in those states—just as railroads running through different states are forced to operate under separate state charters. To perfect the pipe-line system of transportation required many millions of capital. The entire oil business is dependent upon the pipe-line. Without it every well would be less valuable and every market at home and abroad would be more difficult to serve or retain, because of the additional cost to the consumer. The expansion of the whole industry would have been retarded without this method of transportation.

Then the pipe-line system required other improvements, such as tank-cars upon railroads, and finally the tank-steamer. Capital had to be furnished for them and corporations created to own and operate them.

Every one of the steps taken was necessary if the business was to be properly developed, and only through such successive steps and by a great aggregation of capital is America to-day enabled to utilize the bounty which its land pours forth, and to furnish the world with light.

THE START OF THE STANDARD OIL COMPANY

In the year 1867 the firms of William Rockefeller & Co., Rockefeller & Andrews, Rockefeller & Co., and S.V. Harkness and H.M. Flagler united in forming the firm of Rockefeller, Andrews & Flagler.

The cause leading to the formation of this firm was the desire to unite our skill and capital in order to carry on a business of greater magnitude with economy and efficiency in place of the smaller business that each had heretofore conducted separately. As time went on and the possibilities became apparent, we found further capital to be necessary; then we interested others and organized the Standard Oil Company, with a capital of $1,000,000. Later we saw that more money could be utilized, found persons who were willing to invest with us, and increased our capital to $2,500,000, in 1872, and afterward in 1874 to $3,500,000. As the business grew, and markets were obtained at home and abroad, more persons and capital were added to the business, and new corporate agencies were obtained or organized, the object being always the same—to extend our operations by furnishing the best and cheapest products.

I ascribe the success of the Standard Oil Company to its consistent policy of making the volume of its business large through the merit and cheapness of its products. It has spared no expense in utilizing the best and most efficient method of manufacture. It has sought for the best superintendents and workmen and paid the best wages. It has not hesitated to sacrifice old machinery and old plants for new and better ones. It has placed its manufactories at the points where they could supply markets at the least expense. It has not only sought markets for its principal products, but for all possible by-products, sparing no expense in introducing them to the public in every nook and corner of the world. It has not hesitated to invest millions of dollars in methods for cheapening the gathering and distribution of oils by pipe-lines, special cars, tank-steamers, and tank-wagons. It has erected tank-stations at railroad centres in every part of the country to cheapen the storage and delivery of oil. It has had faith in American oil and has brought together vast sums of money for the purpose of making it what it is, and for holding its market against the competition of Russia and all the countries which are producers of oil and competitors against American products.

THE INSURANCE PLANS

Here is an example of one of the ways in which we achieved certain economies and gained real advantage. Fires are always to be reckoned with in oil refining and storage, as we learned by dear experience, but in having our plants distributed all over the country the unit of risk and possible loss was minimized. No one fire could ruin us, and we were able thus to establish a system of insuring ourselves. Our reserve fund which provided for this insurance could not be wiped out all at once, as might be the case with a concern having its plants together or near each other. Then we studied and perfected our organization to prevent fires, improving our appliances and plans year after year until the profit on this insurance feature became a very considerable item in the Standard earnings.

It can easily be seen that this saving in insurance, and minimizing the loss by fire affected the profits, not only in refining, but touched many other associated enterprises: the manufacture of by-products, the tanks and steamers, the pumping-stations, etc.

We devoted ourselves exclusively to the oil business and its products. The company never went into outside ventures, but kept to the enormous task of perfecting its own organization. We educated our own men; we trained many of them from boyhood; we strove to keep them loyal by providing them full scope for their ability; they were given opportunities to buy stock, and the company itself helped them to finance their purchases. Not only here in America, but all over the world, our young men were given chances to advance themselves, and the sons of the old partners were welcomed to the councils and responsibilities of the administration. I may say that the company has been in all its history, and I am sure it is at present, a most happy association of busy people.

I have been asked if my advice is not often sought by the present managers. I can say that if it were sought it would be gladly given. But the fact is that since I retired it has been very little required. I am still a large stockholder, indeed I have increased my holdings in the company's stock since I relinquished any part in its management.

WHY THE STANDARD PAYS LARGE DIVIDENDS

Let me explain what many people, perhaps, fully appreciate, but some, I am sure, do not. The Standard pays four dividends a year: the first in March, which is the result of the busiest season of the whole twelvemonth, because more oil is consumed in winter than at other seasons, and three other dividends later, at about evenly divided periods. Now, these dividends run up to 40 per cent. on the capital stock of $100,000,000, but that does not mean that the profit is 40 per cent. on the capital invested. As a matter of fact, it represents the results of the savings and surplus gained through all the thirty-five or forty years of the workings of the companies. The capital stock could be raised several hundred per cent. without a penny of over-capitalization or "water"; the actual value is there. If this increase had been made, the rate would represent a moderate dividend-paying power of about 6 to 8 per cent.

A NORMAL GROWTH

Study for a moment the result of what has been a natural and absolutely normal increase in the value of the company's possessions. Many of the pipe-lines were constructed during a period when costs were about 50 per cent. of what they are now. Great fields of oil lands were purchased as virgin soil, which later yielded an immense output. Quantities of low-grade crude oil which had been bought by the company when it was believed to be of little value, but which the company hoped eventually to utilize, were greatly increased in value by inventions for refining it and for using the residues formerly considered almost worthless. Dock property was secured at low prices and made valuable by buildings and development. Large unimproved tracts of land near the important business centers were acquired. We brought our industries to these places, made the land useful, and increased the value, not only of our own property, but of the land adjacent to it to many times the original worth. Wherever we have established businesses in this and other countries we have bought largely of property. I remember a case where we paid only $1,000 or so an acre for some rough land to be used for such purposes, and, through the improvements we created, the value has gone up 40 or 50 times as much in 35 or 40 years.

Others have had similar increases in the value of their properties, but have enlarged their capitalization correspondingly. They have escaped the criticism which has been directed against us, who with our old-fashioned and conservative notions have continued without such expansion of capitalization.

There is nothing strange or miraculous in all this; it was all done through this natural law of trade development. It is what the Astors and many other large landholders did.

If a man starts in business with $1,000 capital and gradually increases his property and investment by retaining in his concern much of his earnings, instead of spending them, and thus accumulates values until his investment is, say, $10,000, it would be folly to base the percentage of his actual profits only on the original $1,000 with which he started. Here, again, I think the managers of the Standard should be praised, and not blamed. They have set an example for upbuilding on the most conservative lines, and in a business which has always been, to say the least, hazardous, and to a large degree unavoidably speculative. Yet no one who has relied upon the ownership of this stock to pay a yearly income has been disappointed, and the stock is held by an increasing number of small holders the country over.

THE MANAGEMENT OF CAPITAL

We never attempted, as I have already said, to sell the Standard Oil stock on the market through the Stock Exchange. In the early days the risks of the business were great, and if the stock had been dealt in on the Exchange its fluctuations would no doubt have been violent. We preferred to have the attention of the owners and administrators of the business directed wholly to the legitimate development of the enterprise rather than to speculation in its shares.

The interests of the company have been carefully conserved. We have been criticized for paying large dividends on a capitalization which represents but a small part of the actual property owned by the company. If we had increased the capitalization to bring it up to the real value, and listed the shares on the Exchange, we might have been criticized then for promoting a project to induce the public to invest.

As I have indicated, the foundations of the company were so thoroughly established, and its affairs so conservatively managed, that, after the earlier period of struggle to secure adequate capital and in view of the trying experiences through which we then passed, we decided to pursue the policy of relying upon our own resources. Since then, we have never been obliged to lean very heavily upon the financial public, but have sought rather to hold ourselves in position not only to protect our own large and important interests, but to be prepared in times of stress to lend a helping hand to others. The company has suffered from the statements of people who, I am convinced, are not familiar with all the facts. As I long ago ceased to have any active part in the management of its affairs perhaps, I may venture the opinion that men who devote themselves to building up the sale of American products all over the world, in competition with foreign manufacturers should be appreciated and encouraged.

There have been so many tales told about the so-called speculations of the Standard Oil Company that I may say a word about that subject. This company is interested only in oil products and such manufacturing affairs as are legitimately connected therewith. It has plants for the making of barrels and tanks; and building pumps for pumping oil; it owns vessels for carrying oil, tank-cars, pipes for transporting oil, etc., etc.—but it is not concerned in speculative interests. The oil business itself is speculative enough, and its successful administration requires a firm hand and a cool head.

The company pays dividends to its stockholders which it earns in carrying on this oil trade. This money the stockholders can and do use as they think fit, but the company is in no way responsible for the disposition that the stockholders make of their dividends. The Standard Oil Company does not own or control "a chain of banks," nor has it any interest directly or indirectly in any bank. Its relations are confined to the functions of ordinary banking, such as other depositors have. It buys and sells its own exchange; and these dealings, extending over many years, have made its bills of exchange acceptable all over the world.

CHARACTER THE ESSENTIAL THING

In speaking of the real beginning of the Standard Oil Company, it should be remembered that it was not so much the consolidation of the firms in which we had a personal interest, but the coming together of the men who had the combined brain power to do the work, which was the actual starting-point. Perhaps it is worthwhile to emphasize again the fact that it is not merely capital and "plants" and the strictly material things which make up a business, but the character of the men behind these things, their personalities, and their abilities; these are the essentials to be reckoned with.

Late in 1871, we began the purchase of some of the more important of the refinery interests of Cleveland. The conditions were so chaotic and uncertain that most of the refiners were very desirous to get out of the business. We invariably offered those who wanted to sell the option of taking cash or stock in the company. We very much preferred to have them take the stock, because a dollar in those days looked as large as a cart-wheel, but as a matter of business policy we found it desirable to offer them the option, and in most cases, they were even precipitate in their choice of the cash. They knew what a dollar would buy, but they were very skeptical in regard to the possibilities of resurrecting the oil business and giving any permanent value to these shares.

These purchases continued over a period of years, during which many of the more important refineries at Cleveland were bought by the Standard Oil Company. Some of the smaller concerns, however, continued in the business for many years, although they had the same opportunity as others to sell. There were always, at other refining points which were regarded as more favorably located than Cleveland, many refineries in successful operation.

THE BACKUS PURCHASE

All these purchases of refineries were conducted with the utmost fairness and good faith on our part, yet in many quarters the stories of certain of these transactions have been told in such form as to give the impression that the sales were made most unwillingly and only because the sellers were forced to make them by the most ruthless exertion of superior power.

There was one transaction, viz., the purchase of the property of the Backus Oil Company, which has been variously exploited, and I am made to appear as having personally robbed a defenceless widow of an extremely valuable property, paying her therefor only a mere fraction of its worth.

The story as told is one which makes the strongest appeal to the sympathy and, if it were true, would represent a shocking instance of cruelty in crushing a defenceless woman. It is probable that its wide circulation and its acceptance as true by those who know nothing of the facts has awakened more hostility against the Standard Oil Company and against me personally than any charge which has been made.

This is my reason for entering so much into detail in this particular case, which I am exceedingly reluctant to do, and for many years have refrained from doing.

Mr. F.M. Backus, a highly respected citizen of Cleveland and an old and personal friend of mine, had for several years prior to his death in 1874 been engaged in the lubricating oil business which was carried on after his death as a corporation known as the Backus Oil Company. In the latter part of 1878, our company purchased certain portions of the property of this company. The negotiations which led to this purchase extended over several weeks, being conducted on behalf of Mrs. Backus, as the principal stockholder, by Mr. Charles H. Marr, and on behalf of our company by Mr. Peter S. Jennings. I personally had nothing to do with the negotiations except that, when the matter first came up, Mrs. Backus requested me to call at her house, which I did, when she spoke of selling the property to our company and requested me to personally conduct the negotiations with her with reference to it.

This I was obliged to decline to do, because, as I then explained to her, I was not familiar with the details of the business. In that conversation I advised her not to take any hasty action, and when she expressed fears about the future of the business, stating, for example, that she could not get cars to transport sufficient oil, I said to her that, though we were using our cars and required them in our business, yet we would loan her any number she needed, and do anything else in reason to assist her, and I did not see why she could not successfully prosecute her business in the future as in the past.

I told her, however, that if after reflection she desired to pursue negotiations for the sale of her property some of our people, familiar with the lubricating oil business, would take up the question with her. As she still expressed a desire to have our company buy her property, negotiations were taken up by Mr. Jennings, and the only other thing that I had to do with the matter was that when our experts reported that in their judgment the value of the works, good will, and successorship which we had decided to buy were worth a certain sum, I asked them to add $10,000, in order to make doubly sure that she received full value. The sale was consummated, as we supposed, to the entire satisfaction of Mrs. Backus, and the purchase price which had been agreed upon was paid.

To my profound astonishment, a day or two after the transaction had been closed, I received from her a very unkind letter complaining that she had been unjustly treated. After investigating the matter I wrote her the following letter:

November 13, 1878.

Dear Madam:

I have held your note of the 11th inst., received yesterday, until to-day, as I wished to thoroughly review every point connected with the negotiations for the purchase of the stock of the Backus Oil Company, to satisfy myself as to whether I had unwittingly done anything whereby you could have any right to feel injured. It is true that in the interview I had with you I suggested that if you desired to do so, you could retain an interest in the business of the Backus Oil Company, by keeping some number of its shares, and then I understood you to say that if you sold out you wished to go entirely out of the business.

That being my understanding, our arrangements were made in case you concluded to make the sale that precluded any other interests being represented, and therefore, when you did make the inquiry as to your taking some of the stock, our answer was given in accordance with the facts noted above, but not at all in the spirit in which you refer to the refusal in your note. In regard to the reference that you make as to my permitting the business of the Backus Oil Company to *be taken* from you, I say that in this as in all else you have written in your letter of the 11th inst., you do me most grievous wrong.

It was but of little moment to the interests represented by me whether the business of the Backus Oil Company was purchased or not. I believe that it was for your interest to make the sale, and am entirely candid in this statement, and beg to call your attention to the time, some two years ago, when you consulted Mr. Flagler and myself as to selling out your interests to Mr. Rose, at which time you were desirous of selling at *considerably less price*, and upon time, than you have now received in cash, and which sale you would have been glad to have closed if you could have obtained satisfactory security for the deferred payments.

As to the price paid for the property, it is certainly three times greater than the cost at which we could now construct equal or better facilities; but wishing to take a liberal view of it, I urged the proposal of paying $60,000, which was thought much too high by some of our parties. I believe that if you would reconsider what you have written in your letter, to which this is a reply, you must admit having done me great injustice, and I am satisfied to await upon your innate sense of right for such admission. However, in view of what seems to be your present feeling, I now offer to restore to you the purchase made by us, you simply returning the amount of money which we have invested, and leaving us as though no purchase has been made.

Should you not desire to accept this proposal, I offer to you 100, 200 or 300 shares of the stock at the same price that we paid for the same, with this addition, that if we keep the property we are under engagement to pay into the treasury of the Backus Oil Company any amount which added to the amount already paid would make a total of $100,000 and thereby make the shares $100 each.

That you may not be compelled to hastily come to a conclusion, I will leave open for three days these propositions for your acceptance or declination, and in the meantime believe me,

Yours very truly,

John D. Rockefeller.

Neither of these offers was accepted. In order that this may not rest on my unsupported assertion, I submit the following documents: The first is a letter from Mr. H.M. Backus, a brother of Mrs. Backus's deceased husband, who had been associated with the business and had remained with the company after his death. The letter was written without any solicitation whatever on my part, but I have since received permission from Mr. Backus to print it. It is followed by extracts from affidavits made by the gentleman who conducted the negotiations on behalf of Mrs. Backus. I have no wish to reprint the complimentary allusion to myself in Mr. Backus's letter, but have feared to omit a word of it lest some misunderstanding ensue:

Bowling Green, Ohio,
September 18, '03.

Mr. John D. Rockefeller,
Cleveland, Ohio.

I do not know whether you will ever receive this letter or not, whether your secretary will throw it into the waste-basket or not, but I will do my part and get it off my mind, and it will not be my fault if you do not receive or read it. Ever since the day that my deceased brother's wife, Mrs. F.N. Backus, wrote you the unjust and unreasonable letter in reference to the sale of the property of the old Backus Oil Company, in which I had a small interest, I have wanted to write you and record my disapproval of that letter. I lived with my brother's family, was at the house the day you called to talk the matter of the then proposed purchase of the property with Mrs. Backus by her request, as she told Mr. Jennings that she wanted to deal through you. I was in favor of the sale from the first.

I was with Mrs. Backus all through the trouble with Mr. Rose and with Mr. Maloney, did what I could to encourage her, and to prevent Mr. Rose from getting the best of her. Mrs. Backus, in my opinion, is an exceptionally good financier, but she does not know and no one can convince her that the best thing that ever happened to her financially was the sale of her interest in the Backus Oil Company to your people. She does not know that five more years of the then increasing desperate competition would have bankrupted the company, and that with the big debt that she was carrying on the lot on Euclid Avenue, near Sheriff Street, she would have been swamped, and that the only thing that ever saved her and the oil business generally was the plan of John D. Rockefeller. She thinks that you literally robbed her of millions, and feeds her children on that diet three times a day more or less, principally more, until it has become a mania with her, and no argument that any one else can suggest will have any effect upon her. She is wise and good in many ways, but on that one subject she is one-sided, I think. Of course, if we could have been assured of continued dividends, I would have been opposed to selling the business, but that was out of the question. I know of the ten thousand dollars that was added to the purchase price of the property at your request, and I know that you paid three times the value of the property, and I know that all that ever saved our company from ruin was the sale of its property to you, and I simply want to ease my mind by doing justice to you by saying so. After the sale to your company I was simple enough to go to Buffalo and try it again, but soon met with defeat and retired with my flag in the dust. I then went to Duluth, and was on the top wave, till the real-estate bubble broke, and I broke with it. I have had my ups and downs, but I have tried to take my medicine and look pleasant instead of sitting down under a juniper tree and blaming my losses to John D. Rockefeller.

I suppose I would have put off writing this letter for another year or more as I have done so long, had it not been for a little chat that I had with Mr. Hanafin, Superintendent of the Buckeye Pipe Line

Company, a day or two since when I was relating the sale, etc., of the old B.O. Co.'s business, and in that way revived the intention that had lain dormant since the last good resolution in regard to writing it was made. But it's done now, and off my mind.

With much respect and admiration to John D. Rockefeller I remain,

Yours truly,

H.M. Backus.

It appears from the affidavits that the negotiations were conducted on behalf of Mrs. Backus and her company by Charles H. Marr, who had been in the employ of the Backus Company for some time, and by Mr. Maloney, who was the superintendent of the company from the time of its organization and was also a stockholder; and on behalf of the Standard Oil Company by Mr. Peter S. Jennings.

There has been an impression that the Standard Oil Company purchased for $79,000 property which was reasonably worth much more, and that this sacrifice was occasioned by threats and compulsion. Mr. Jennings requested Mr. Marr to submit a written proposition giving the price put by the Backus Company upon the several items of property and assets which it desired to sell. This statement was furnished and was annexed to Mr. Jennings's affidavit. The Standard Oil Company finally decided not to purchase all of the assets of the company, but only the oil on hand, for which it paid the full market price, amounting to about $19,000, and the item "works, good-will, and successorship," which were offered by Mr. Marr at $71,000, and for which the

Standard offered $60,000, which was promptly accepted. Mr. Marr made affidavit as follows:

"Charles H. Marr, being duly sworn, says that, in behalf of the Backus Oil Company, he conducted the negotiations which led to the sale of its works, good-will, and stock of oils and during same when said company had offered to sell its entire stock for a gross sum, to wit, the sum of one hundred and fifty thousand dollars ($150,000), which was to include cash on hand, accrued dividends, accounts, etc., said Jennings requested said company to submit an itemized proposition fixing values upon different articles proposed to be sold, and that he, after full consideration with Mrs. Backus and with her knowledge and consent, submitted the written proposition attached to said Jennings's affidavit; that the same is in his handwriting, and was copied at the office of the American Lubricating Oil Company from the original by himself at the request of said Jennings, and said original was submitted by affiant to Mrs. Backus.

"That she was fully cognizant of all the details of said negotiations and the items and values attached thereto in said proposition, consulted with at every step thereof, none of which were taken without her advice, as she was by far the largest stockholder in said Backus Oil Company, owning about seven-tenths (7/10) of said company's stock, and she fully approved of said proposition, and accepted the offer of said Jennings to pay sixty thousand dollars ($60,000) for the item works, good-will, and successorship without any opposition, so far as affiant knows. And affiant says that the amount realized from the assets of the Backus Oil Company, including purchase price, has been about one hundred and thirty-three thousand dollars ($133,000), and a part of its assets have not yet been converted into money as affiant is informed."

Mr. Marr, who was, it will be remembered, the widow's representative, refers to the negotiations leading up to the purchase and says:

"But affiant says that nothing that was said by Mr. Jennings or anybody else during their progress could be construed into a threat, nor did anything that was said or done by said Jennings hasten or push forward said trade."

He also says:

"Affiant says that the negotiations extended over a period of from two to three weeks ... and during their pendency that Mrs. Backus frequently urged affiant to bring the same to a conclusion as she was anxious to dispose of said business and relieve herself from further care and responsibility therewith. And when the said offer of purchase by said Jennings upon the terms aforesaid was conveyed to her by affiant, she expressed herself as entirely satisfied therewith."

Mr. Maloney made an affidavit that he was superintendent of the Backus Oil Company from the time of its organization, and also a stockholder in the company, and had been associated in business with Mr. Backus for many years previous to his death; that he took part in the negotiations for the sale, representing Mrs. Backus in the matter. After speaking of the negotiations, he says:

"Finally, after consultation, the proposition was made by her to dispose of the works, good-will, and successorship for $71,000. A few days after the proposal was made to her to pay the sum of $60,000 for works and good-will, and to take the oil on hand at its market price, which proposition she accepted, and the sale was concluded.

"During these negotiations Mrs. Backus was anxious to sell, and was entirely satisfied with the sale after it was concluded. I know of the fact that about a year and a half previous she had offered to sell out the stock of the Backus Oil Company at from 30 to 33 per cent. less than she received in the sale referred to, and the value of the works and property sold had not increased in the meantime. I was well acquainted with the works of the Backus Oil Company and their value. I could at the time of the sale have built the works new for $25,000. There were no threats nor intimidations, nor anything of the kind used to force the sale. The negotiations were pleasant and fair, and the price paid in excess of the value, and satisfactory to Mrs. Backus and all concerned for her."

So far as I can see, after more than 30 years have elapsed, there was nothing but the most kindly and considerate treatment of Mrs. Backus on the part of the Standard Oil Company. I regret that Mrs. Backus did not take at least part of her pay in Standard certificates, as we suggested she should do.

THE QUESTION OF REBATES

Of all the subjects which seem to have attracted the attention of the public to the affairs of the Standard Oil Company, the matter of rebates from railroads has perhaps been uppermost. The Standard Oil Company of Ohio, of which I was president, did receive rebates from the railroads prior to 1880, but received no advantages for which it did not give full compensation. The reason for rebates was that such was the railroads' method of business. A public rate was made and collected by the railroad companies, but, so far as my knowledge extends, was seldom retained in full; a portion of it was repaid to the shippers as a rebate. By this method the real rate of freight which any shipper paid was not known by his competitors nor by other railroad companies, the amount being a matter of bargain with the carrying company. Each shipper made the best bargain that he could, but whether he was doing better than his competitor was only a matter of conjecture.

Much depended upon whether the shipper had the advantage of competition of carriers.

The Standard Oil Company of Ohio, being situated at Cleveland, had the advantage of different carrying lines, as well as of water transportation in the summer; taking advantage of those facilities, it made the best bargains possible for its freights. Other companies sought to do the same. The Standard gave advantages to the railroads for the purpose of reducing the cost of transportation of freight. It offered freights in large quantity, car-loads and train-loads. It furnished loading facilities and discharging facilities at great cost. It provided regular traffic, so that a railroad could conduct its transportation to the best advantage and use its equipment to the full extent of its hauling capacity without waiting for the refiner's convenience. It exempted railroads from liability for fire and carried its own insurance. It provided at its own expense terminal facilities which permitted economies in handling. For these services it obtained contracts for special allowances on freights.

But notwithstanding these special allowances, this traffic from the Standard Oil Company was far more profitable to the railroad companies than the smaller and irregular traffic, which might have paid a higher rate.

To understand the situation which affected the giving and taking of rebates it must be remembered that the railroads were all eager to enlarge their freight traffic. They were competing with the facilities and rates offered by the boats on lake and canal and by the pipe-lines. All these means of transporting oil cut into the business of the railroads, and they were desperately anxious to successfully meet this competition. As I have stated we provided means for loading and unloading cars expeditiously, agreed to furnish a regular fixed number of car-loads to transport each day, and arranged with them for all the other things that I have mentioned, the final result being to reduce the cost of transportation for both the railroads and ourselves. All this was following in the natural laws of trade.

PIPE-LINES VS. RAILROADS

The building of the pipe-lines introduced another formidable competitor to the railroads, but as oil could be transported by pumping through pipes at a much less cost than by hauling in tank-cars in a railroad train the development of the pipe-line was inevitable. The question was simply whether the oil traffic was sufficient in volume to make the investment profitable. When pipe-lines had been built to oil fields where the wells had ceased to yield, as often happened, they were about the most useless property imaginable.

An interesting feature developed through the relations which grew up between the railroads and the pipe-lines. In many cases it was necessary to combine the facilities of both, because the pipes reached only part of the way, and from the place where they ended the railroad carried the oil to its final destination. In some instances, a railroad had formerly carried the oil the entire distance upon an agreed rate, but now that this oil was partly pumped by pipe-lines and partly carried by rail, the freight payment was divided between the two. But, as a through rate had been provided, the owners of the pipe-line agreed to remit a part of its charges to the railroad, so we had cases where the Standard paid a rebate to the railroad instead of the reverse—but I do not remember having heard any complaint of this coming from the students of these complicated subjects.

The profits of the Standard Oil Company did not come from advantages given by railroads. The railroads, rather, were the ones who profited by the traffic of the Standard Oil Company, and whatever advantage it received in its constant efforts to reduce rates of freight was only one of the many elements of lessening cost to the consumer which enabled us to increase our volume of business the world over because we could reduce the selling price.

How general was the complicated bargaining for rates can hardly be imagined; everyone got the best rate that he could. After the passage of the Interstate Commerce Act, it was learned that many small companies which shipped limited quantities had received lower rates than we had been able to secure, notwithstanding the fact that we had made large investments to provide for terminal facilities, regular shipments, and other economies. I well remember a bright man from Boston who had much to say about rebates and drawbacks. He was an old and experienced merchant, and looked after his affairs with a cautious and watchful eye. He feared that some of his competitors were doing better than he in bargaining for rates, and he delivered himself of this conviction:

"I am opposed on principle to the whole system of rebates and drawbacks—unless I am in it."

CHAPTER V

Other Business Experiences and Business Principles

Going into the iron-ore fields was one of those experiences in which one finds oneself rather against the will, for it was not a deliberate plan of mine to extend my cares and responsibilities. My connection with iron ores came about through some unfortunate investments in the Northwest country.

These interests had included a good many different industries, mines, steel mills, paper mills, a nail factory, railroads, lumber fields, smelting properties, and other investments about which I have now forgotten. I was a minority stockholder in all these enterprises, and had no part in their management. Not all of them were profitable. As a matter of fact, for a period of years just preceding the panic of 1893, values were more or less inflated, and many people who thought they were wealthy found that the actual facts were quite different from what they had imagined when the hard experiences of that panic forced upon them the unpalatable truth.

Most of these properties I had not even seen, having relied upon the investigation of others respecting their worth; indeed, it has never been my custom to rely alone upon my own knowledge of the value of such plants. I have found other people who knew much better than I how to investigate such enterprises.

Even at this time I had been planning to relieve myself of business cares, and the panic only caused me to postpone taking the long holiday to which I had been looking forward. I was fortunate in making the acquaintance of Mr. Frederick T. Gates, who was then engaged in some work in connection with the American Baptist Education Society, which required him to travel extensively over the country, north, south, east, and west.

It occurred to me that Mr. Gates, who had a great store of common sense, though no especial technical information about factories and mills, might aid me in securing some first-hand information as to how these concerns were actually prospering. Once, as he was going South, I suggested that he look over an iron mill in which I had some interest which happened to be on his route.

His report was a model of what such a report should be. It stated the facts, and in this case they were almost all unfavourable. A little later he happened to be going West, and I gave him the name and address of property in that region in which I held a minority interest. I felt quite sure that this particular property was doing well, and it was somewhat of a shock to me to learn through his clear and definite account that it was only a question of time before this enterprise, too, which had been represented as rolling in money, would get into trouble if things kept on as they were going.

NURSING THE COMMERCIALLY ILL

I then arranged with Mr. Gates to accept a position whereby he could help me unravel these tangled affairs, and become, like myself, a man of business, but it was agreed between us that he should not abandon his larger and more important plans for working out some philanthropic aspirations that he had.

Right here I may stop to give credit to Mr. Gates for possessing a combination of rare business ability, very highly developed and very honorably exercised, overshadowed by a passion to accomplish some great and far-reaching benefits to mankind, the influence of which will last. He is the chairman of the General Education Board and active in many other boards, and for years he has helped in the various plans that we have been interested in where money was given in the hope that it would do something more than temporary service.

Mr. Gates has for many years been closely associated with my personal affairs. He has been through strenuous times with me, and has taken cares of many kinds off my shoulders, leaving me more time to play golf, plan roads, move trees, and follow other congenial occupations. His efforts in the investigations in connection with our educational contributions, our medical research, and other kindred works have been very successful. During the last ten or twelve years my son has shared with Mr. Gates the responsibility of this work, and more recently Mr. Starr J. Murphy has also joined with us to help Mr. Gates, who has borne the heat and burden of the day, and has well earned some leisure which we have wanted him to enjoy.

But to return to the story of our troubled investments: Mr. Gates went into the study of each of these business concerns, and did the best he could with them. It has been our policy never to allow a company in which we had an interest to be thrown into the bankruptcy court if we could prevent it; for receiverships are very costly in many ways and often involve heavy sacrifices of genuine values. Our plan has been to stay with the institution, nurse it, lend it money when necessary, improve facilities, cheapen production, and avail ourselves of the opportunities which time and patience are likely to bring to make it self-sustaining and successful. So we went carefully through the affairs of these crippled enterprises in the hard times of 1893 and 1894, carrying many of them for years after; sometimes buying the interests of others and sometimes selling our own interest, but all or nearly all escaped the expenses and humiliation of bankruptcy, receivership, and foreclosure.

Before these matters were entirely closed up we had a vast amount of experience in the doctoring of the commercially ill. My only excuse for dwelling upon the subject at this late day is to point out the fact to some business men who get discouraged that much can be done by careful and patient attention, even when the business is apparently in very deep water. It requires two things: some added capital, put in by one's self or secured from others, and a strict adherence to the sound natural laws of business.

THE ORE MINES

Among these investments were some shares in a number of ore mines and an interest in the stocks and bonds of a railroad being built to carry the ore from the mines to lake ports. We had great faith in these mines, but to work them the railroad was necessary. It had been begun, but in the panic of 1893 it and all other developments were nearly ruined. Although we were minority holders of the stock, it seemed to be "up to us" to keep the enterprise alive through the harrowing panic days. I had to loan my personal securities to raise money, and finally we were compelled to supply a great deal of actual cash, and to get it we were obliged to go into the then greatly upset money market and buy currency at a high premium to ship west by express to pay the laborers on the railroad and to keep them alive. When the fright of the panic period subsided, and matters became a little more settled, we began to realize our situation. We had invested many millions, and no one wanted to go in with us to buy stock. On the contrary, everybody else seemed to want to sell. The stock was offered to us in alarming quantities—substantially all of the capital stock of the companies came without any solicitation on our part— quite the contrary—and we paid for it in cash.

We now found ourselves in control of a great amount of ore lands, from some of which the ore could be removed by a steam shovel for a few cents a ton, but we still faced a most imperfect and inadequate method of transporting the ore to market.

When we realized that events were shaping themselves so that to protect our investments we should be obliged to go into the business of selling in a large way, we felt that we must not stop short of doing the work as effectively as possible; and having already put in so much money, we bought all the ore land that we thought was good that was offered to us. The railroad and the ships were only a means to an end. The ore lands were the crux of the whole matter, and we believed that we could never have too many good mines.

It was a surprise to me that the great iron and steel manufacturers did not place what seemed to be an adequate value on these mines. The lands which contained a good many of our best ore mines could have been purchased very cheaply before we became interested. Having launched ourselves into the venture, we decided to supply ore to every one who needed it, by mining and transporting with the newest and most effective facilities, and our profits we invested in more ore lands.

Mr. Gates became the president of the various companies which owned the mines and the railroad to the lake to transport the ores, and he started to learn and develop the business of ore mining and transportation. He not only proved to be an apt scholar, but he really mastered the various complexities of the business. He did all the work, and only consulted me when he wished to; yet I remember several interesting experiences connected with the working out of these problems.

BUILDING THE SHIPS

After this railroad problem was solved, it was apparent that we needed our own ships to transport the ore down the lakes. We knew absolutely nothing of building ships for ore transportation, and so, following out our custom, we went to the man who, in our judgment, had the widest knowledge of the subject. He was already well known to us, but was in the ore transportation business on a large scale on his own account and, of course, the moment we began to ship ore we realized that we would become competitors. Mr. Gates got into communication with this expert, and came with him one evening to my house in New York just before dinner. He said he could stay only a few minutes, but I told him that I thought we could finish up our affairs in ten minutes and we did. This is the only time I remember seeing personally any one on the business of the ore company. All the conferences, as I said before, were carried on by Mr. Gates, who seemed to enjoy work, and he has had abundant privileges in that direction.

We explained to this gentleman that we were proposing to transport our ore from these Lake Superior lands ourselves, and that we should like to have him assume charge of the construction of several ships, to be of the largest and most approved type, for our chance of success lay in having boats which could be operated with the greatest efficiency. At that time the largest ships carried about five thousand tons, but in 1900, when we sold out, we had ships that carried seven thousand or eight thousand tons, and now there are some that transport as much as ten thousand tons and more.

This expert naturally replied that as he was in the ore-carrying trade himself, he had no desire to encourage us to go into it. We explained to him that as we had made this large investment, it seemed to us to be necessary for the protection of our interests to control our own lake carriers, so we had decided to mine, ship, and market the ore; that we came to him because he could plan and superintend the construction of the best ships for us, and that we wanted to deal with him for that reason; that notwithstanding that he represented one of the largest firms among our competitors, we knew that he was honest and straightforward; and that we were most anxious to deal with him.

EMPLOYING A COMPETITOR

He still demurred, but we tried to convince him that we were not to be deterred from going into the trade, and that we were willing to pay him a satisfactory commission for looking after the building of the ships. Somebody, we explained, was going to do the work for us, and he might as well have the profit as the next man. This argument finally seemed to impress him and we then and there closed an agreement, the details of which were worked out afterward to our mutual satisfaction. This gentleman was Mr. Samuel Mather of Cleveland. He spent only a few minutes in the house, during which time we gave him the order for about

$3,000,000 worth of ships and this was the only time I saw him. But Mr. Mather is a man of high business honor, we trusted him implicitly although he was a competitor, and we never had occasion to regret it.

At that time there were some nine or ten shipbuilding companies located at various points on the Great Lakes. All were independent of each other and there was sharp competition between them. Times were pretty hard with them; their business had not yet recovered from the panic of 1893, they were not able to keep their works in full operation; it was in the fall of the year and many of their employees were facing a hard winter. We took this into account in considering how many ships we should build, and we made up our minds that we would build all the ships that could be built and give employment to the idle men on the Great Lakes.

Accordingly, we instructed Mr. Mather to write to each firm of shipbuilders and ascertain how many ships they could build and put in readiness for operation at the opening of navigation the next spring. He found that some companies could build one, some could build two, and that the total number would be twelve. Accordingly, we asked him to have constructed twelve ships, all of steel, all of the largest capacity then understood to be practicable on the Great Lakes. Some of them were to be steamships and some consorts, for towing, but all were to be built on substantially the same general pattern, which was to represent the best ideals then prevalent for ore-carrying ships.

In giving such an order he was exposed, of course, to the risk of paying very high prices. This would have been certain if Mr. Mather had announced in advance that he was prepared to build twelve ships and asked bids on them. Just how he managed it I was not told until long after, and though it is now an old story of the lakes I repeat it as it may be new to many. Mr. Mather kept the secret of the number of ships he wished to construct absolutely to himself. He sent his plans and specifications, each substantially a duplicate of the others, to each of the firms, and asked each firm to bid on one or two ships as the case might be. All naturally supposed that at most only two ships were to be built, and each was extremely eager to get the work, or at least one of the two vessels.

On the day before the contracts were to be let, all the bidders were in Cleveland on the invitation of Mr. Mather. One by one they were taken into his private office for special conference covering all the details preparatory to the final bid. At the appointed hour the bids were in. Deep was the interest on the part of all the gentlemen as to who would be the lucky one to draw the prize. Mr. Mather's manner had convinced each that somehow, he himself must be the favored bidder, yet when he came to meet his competitors in the hotel lobby the beams of satisfaction which plainly emanated from their faces also compelled many hearts searching.

At last, the crucial hour came, and at about the same moment each gentleman received a little note from Mr. Mather, conveying to him the tidings that to him had been awarded a contract sufficient to supply his works to their utmost capacity. They all rushed with a common impulse to the hotel lobby where they had been accustomed to meet, each bent on displaying his note and commiserating his unsuccessful rivals, only to discover that each had a contract for all he could do, and that each had been actually bidding against nobody but himself. Great was the hilarity which covered their chagrin when they met and compared notes and looked into each other's' faces. However, all were happy and satisfied. But it may be said in passing that these amiable gentlemen all united subsequently in one company, which has had a highly satisfactory career, and that we paid a more uniform price for our subsequent purchases of ships after the combination had been made.

A LANDSMAN FOR SHIP MANAGER

With these ships ordered, we were fairly at the beginning of the ore enterprise. But we realized that we had to make some arrangement to operate the ships, and we again turned to our competitor, Mr. Mather, in the hope that he would add this to his cares. Unfortunately, because of his obligations to others, he felt that this was impractical. I asked Mr. Gates one day soon after this:

"How are we to get some one to run these big ships we have ordered? Do you know of any experienced firm?"

"No," said Mr. Gates, "I do not know of any firm to suggest at the moment, but why not run them ourselves?"

"You don't know anything about ships, do you?"

"No," he admitted, "but I have in mind a man who I believe could do it, although when I tell you about him I fear you will think that his qualifications are not the best. However, he has the essentials. He lives up the state, and never was on a ship in his life. He probably wouldn't know the bow from the stern, or a sea-anchor from an umbrella, but he has good sense, he is honest, enterprising, keen, and thrifty. He has the art of quickly mastering a subject even though it be new to him and difficult. We still have some months before the ships will be completed, and if we put him to work now, he will be ready to run the ships as soon as they are ready to be run."

"All right," I said, "let's give him the job," and we did.

That man was Mr. L.M. Bowers; he came from Broome County, New York. Mr. Bowers went from point to point on the lakes where the boats were building, and studied them minutely. He was quickly able to make valuable suggestions about their construction, which were approved and adopted by the designers. When the vessels were finished, he took charge of them from the moment they floated, and he managed these and the dozens which followed with a skill and ability that commanded the admiration of all the sailors on the lakes. He even invented an anchor which he used with our fleet, and later it was adopted by other vessels, and I have heard that it is used in the United States Navy. He remained in his position until we sold out. We have given Mr. Bowers all sorts of hard tasks since we retired from the lake traffic and have found him always successful. Lately the health of a member of his family has made it desirable for him to live in Colorado, and he is now the vigorous and efficient vice-president of the Colorado Fuel and Iron Company.

The great ships and the railroad put us in possession of the most favourable facilities. From the first the organization was successful. We built up a huge trade, mining and carrying ore to Cleveland and other lake ports. We kept on building and developing until finally the fleet grew until it included fifty-six large steel vessels, This enterprise, in common with many other important business undertakings in which I was interested, required very little of my personal attention, owing to my good fortune in having active, competent, and thoroughly reliable representatives who assumed so largely the responsibilities of administration. It gives me pleasure to state that the confidence which I have freely given to business men with whom I have been associated has been so fully justified.

SELLING TO THE STEEL COMPANY

The work went on uninterruptedly and prosperously until the formation of the United States Steel Corporation. A representative of this corporation came to see us about selling the land, the ore, and the fleet of ships. The business was going on smoothly, and we had no pressing need to sell, but as the organizer of the new company felt that our mines and railroads and ships were a necessary part of the scheme, we told him we would be pleased to facilitate the completion of the great undertaking. They had, I think, already closed with Mr. Carnegie for his various properties. After some negotiation, they made an offer which we accepted, whereby the whole plant—mines, ships, railway, etc.—should become a part of the United States Steel Corporation. The price paid was, we felt, very moderate considering the present and prospective value of the property.

This transaction bids fair to show a great profit to the Steel Company for many years, and as our payment was largely in the securities of the company we had the opportunity to participate in this prosperity. And so, after a period of about seven years, I went out of all association with the mining, the transporting, and the selling of iron ore.

FOLLOW THE LAWS OF TRADE

Going over again in my mind the events connected with this ore experience that grew out of investments that seemed at the time, to say the least, rather unpromising, I am impressed anew with the importance of a principle I have often referred to. If I can make this point clear to the young man who has had the patience to follow these Reminiscences so far, it will be a satisfaction to me and I hope it may be a benefit to him.

The underlying, essential element of success in business affairs is to follow the established laws of high-class dealing. Keep to broad and sure lines, and study them to be certain that they are correct ones. Watch the natural operations of trade, and keep within them. Don't even think of temporary or sharp advantages. Don't waste your effort on a thing which ends in a petty triumph unless you are satisfied with a life of petty success. Be sure that before you go into an enterprise you see your way clear to stay through to a successful end. Look ahead. It is surprising how many bright business men go into important undertakings with little or no study of the controlling conditions they risk their all upon.

Study diligently your capital requirements, and fortify yourself fully to cover possible set-backs, because you can absolutely count on meeting set-backs. Be sure that you are not deceiving yourself at any time about actual conditions. The man who starts out simply with the idea of getting rich won't succeed; you must have a larger ambition. There is no mystery in business success. The great industrial leaders have told again and again the plain and obvious fact that there can be no permanent success without fair dealing that leads to wide-spread confidence in the man himself, and that is the real capital we all prize and work for. If you do each day's task successfully, and stay faithfully within these natural operations of commercial laws which I talk so much about, and keep your head clear, you will come out all right, and will then, perhaps, forgive me for moralizing in this old-fashioned way. It is hardly necessary to caution a young man who reads so sober a book as this not to lose his head over a little success, or to grow impatient or discouraged by a little failure.

PANIC EXPERIENCES

I had desired to retire from business in the early nineties. Having begun work so young, I felt that at fifty it was due me to have freedom from absorption in active business affairs and to devote myself to a variety of interests other than money making, which had claimed a portion of my time since the beginning of my business career. But 1891-92 were years of ominous outlook. In 1893 the storm broke, and I had many investments to care for, as I have already related. This year and the next was a trying period of grave anxiety to every one. No one could retire from work at such a time. In the Standard we continued to make progress even through all these panic years, as we had large reserves of cash on account of our very conservative methods of financing. In 1894 or 1895 I was able to carry out my plans to be relieved from any association with the actual management of the company's affairs. From that time, as I have said, I have had little or no part in the conduct of the business.

Since 1857 I can remember all the great panics, but I believe the panic of 1907 was the most trying. No one escaped from it, great or small. Important institutions had to be supported and carried through the time of distrust and unreasoning fear. To Mr. Morgan's real and effective help I should join with other business men and give great praise. His commanding personality served a most valuable end. He acted quickly and resolutely when quickness and decision were the things most needed to regain confidence, and he was efficiently seconded by many able and leading financiers of the country who cooperated courageously and effectively to restore confidence and prosperity. The question has been asked if I think we shall revive quickly from the panic of October, 1907. I hesitate to speak on the subject, since I am not a prophet nor the son of a prophet; but as to the ultimate outcome there is, of course, no doubt. This temporary set-back will lead to safer institutions and more conservative management upon the part of every one, and this is a quality we need. It will not long depress our wonderful spirit of initiative. The country's resources have not been cut down nor injured by financial distrust. A gradual recovery will only tend to make the future all the more secure, and patience is a virtue in business affairs as in other things.

Here again I would venture to utter a word of caution to business men. Let them study their own affairs frankly, and face the truth. If their methods are extravagant, let them realize the facts and act accordingly. One cannot successfully go against natural tendencies, and it is folly to fail to recognize them. It is not easy for so impressionable and imaginative a people as we Americans are to come down to plain, hard facts, yet we are doing it without loss of self-esteem or prestige throughout the world.

CHAPTER VI

The Difficult Art of Giving

It is, no doubt, easy to write platitudes and generalities about the joys of giving, and the duty that one owes to one's fellow men, and to put together again all the familiar phrases that have served for generations whenever the subject has been taken up.

I can hardly hope to succeed in starting any new interest in this great subject when gifted writers have so often failed. Yet I confess I find much more interest in it at this time than in rambling on, as I have been doing, about the affairs of business and trade. It is most difficult, however, to dwell upon a very practical and business-like side of benefactions generally, without seeming to ignore, or at least to fail to appreciate fully, the spirit of giving which has its source in the heart, and which, of course, makes it all worthwhile.

In this country we have come to the period when we can well afford to ask the ablest men to devote more of their time, thought, and money to the public well-being. I am not so presumptuous as to attempt to define exactly what this betterment work should consist of. Every man will do that for himself, and his own conclusion will be final for himself. It is well, I think, that no narrow or preconceived plan should be set down as the best.

I am sure it is a mistake to assume that the possession of money in great abundance necessarily brings happiness. The very rich are just like all the rest of us; and if they get pleasure from the possession of money, it comes from their ability to do things which give satisfaction to someone besides themselves.

LIMITATIONS OF THE RICH

The mere expenditure of money for things, so I am told by those who profess to know, soon palls upon one. The novelty of being able to purchase anything one wants soon passes, because what people most seek cannot be bought with money. These rich men we read about in the newspapers cannot get personal returns beyond a well-defined limit for their expenditure. They cannot gratify the pleasures of the palate beyond very moderate bounds, since they cannot purchase a good digestion; they cannot lavish very much money on fine raiment for themselves or their families without suffering from public ridicule; and in their homes they cannot go much beyond the comforts of the less wealthy without involving them in more pain than pleasure. As I study wealthy men, I can see but one way in which they can secure a real equivalent for money spent, and that is to cultivate a taste for giving where the money may produce an effect which will be a lasting gratification.

A man of business may often most properly consider that he does his share in building up a property which gives steady work for few or many people; and his contribution consists in giving to his employees good working conditions, new opportunities, and a strong stimulus to good work. Just so long as he has the welfare of his employees in his mind and follows his convictions, no one can help honoring such a man. It would be the narrowest sort of view to take, and I think the meanest, to consider that good works consist chiefly in the outright giving of money.

THE BEST PHILANTHROPY

The best philanthropy, the help that does the most good and the least harm, the help that nourishes civilization at its very root, that most widely disseminates health, righteousness, and happiness, is not what is usually called charity. It is, in my judgment, the investment of effort or time or money, carefully considered with relation to the power of employing people at a remunerative wage, to expand and develop the resources at hand, and to give opportunity for progress and healthful labor where it did not exist before. No mere money-giving is comparable to this in its lasting and beneficial results.

If, as I am accustomed to think, this statement is a correct one, how vast indeed is the philanthropic field! It may be urged that the daily vocation of life is one thing, and the work of philanthropy quite another. I have no sympathy with this notion. The man who plans to do all his giving on Sunday is a poor prop for the institutions of the country.

The excuse for referring so often to the busy man of affairs is that his help is most needed. I know of men who have followed out this large plan of developing work, not as a temporary matter, but as a permanent principle. These men have taken up doubtful enterprises and carried them through to success often at great risk, and in the face of great scepticism, not as a matter only of personal profit, but in the larger spirit of general uplift.

DISINTERESTED SERVICE THE ROAD TO SUCCESS

If I were to give advice to a young man starting out in life, I should say to him: If you aim for a large, broad-gauged success, do not begin your business career, whether you sell your labor or are an independent producer, with the idea of getting from the world by hook or crook all you can. In the choice of your profession or your business employment, let your first thought be: Where can I fit in so that I may be most effective in the work of the world? Where can I lend a hand in a way most effectively to advance the general interests?

Enter life in such a spirit, choose your vocation in that way, and you have taken the first step on the highest road to a large success.

Investigation will show that the great fortunes which have been made in this country, and the same is probably true of other lands, have come to men who have performed great and far-reaching economic services—men who, with great faith in the future of their country, have done most for the development of its resources. The man will be most successful who confers the greatest service on the world. Commercial enterprises that are needed by the public will pay. Commercial enterprises that are not needed fail, and ought to fail.

On the other hand, the one thing which such a business philosopher would be most careful to avoid in his investments of time and effort or money, is the unnecessary duplication of existing industries. He would regard all money spent in increasing needless competition as wasted, and worse. The man who puts up a second factory when the factory in existence will supply the public demand adequately and cheaply is wasting the national wealth and destroying the national prosperity, taking the bread from the laborer and unnecessarily introducing heartache and misery into the world.

Probably the greatest single obstacle to the progress and happiness of the American people lies in the willingness of so many men to invest their time and money in multiplying competitive industries instead of opening up new fields, and putting their money into lines of industry and development that are needed. It requires a better type of mind to seek out and to support or to create the new than to follow the worn paths of accepted success; but here is the great chance in our still rapidly developing country. The penalty of a selfish attempt to make the world confer a living without contributing to the progress or happiness of mankind is generally a failure to the individual. The pity is that when he goes down he inflicts heartache and misery also on others who are in no way responsible.

THE GENEROSITY OF SERVICE

Probably the most generous people in the world are the very poor, who assume each other's burdens in the crises which come so often to the hard pressed. The mother in the tenement falls ill and the neighbor in the next room assumes her burdens. The father loses his work, and neighbors supply food to his children from their own scanty store. How often one hears of cases where the orphans are taken over and brought up by the poor friend whose benefaction means great additional hardship! This sort of genuine service makes the most princely gift from superabundance look insignificant indeed. The Jews have had for centuries a precept that one-tenth of a man's possessions must be devoted to good works, but even this measure of giving is but a rough yardstick to go by. To give a tenth of one's income is wellnigh an impossibility to some, while to others it means a miserable pittance. If the spirit is there, the matter of proportion is soon lost sight of. It is only the spirit of giving that counts, and the very poor give without any self-consciousness. But I fear that I am dealing with generalities again.

The education of children in my early days may have been straightlaced, yet I have always been thankful that the custom was quite general to teach young people to give systematically of money that they themselves had earned. It is a good thing to lead children to realize early the importance of their obligations to others but, I confess, it is increasingly difficult; for what were luxuries then have become commonplaces now. It should be a greater pleasure and satisfaction to give money for a good cause than to earn it, and I have always indulged the hope that during my life I should be able to help establish efficiency in giving so that wealth may be of greater use to the present and future generations.

Perhaps just here lies the difference between the gifts of money and of service. The poor meet promptly the misfortunes which confront the home circle and household of the neighbor. The giver of money, if his contribution is to be valuable, must add service in the way of study, and he must help to attack and improve underlying conditions. Not being so pressed by the racking necessities, it is he that should be better able to attack the subject from a more scientific standpoint; but the final analysis is the same: his money is a feeble offering without the study behind it which will make its expenditure effective.

Great hospitals conducted by noble and unselfish men and women are doing wonderful work; but no less important are the achievements in research that reveal hitherto unknown facts about diseases and provide the remedies by which many of them can be relieved or even stamped out.

To help the sick and distressed appeals to the kind-hearted always, but to help the investigator who is striving successfully to attack the causes which bring about sickness and distress does not so strongly attract the giver of money. The first appeals to the sentiments overpoweringly, but the second has the head to deal with. Yet I am sure we are making wonderful advances in this field of scientific giving. All over the world the need of dealing with the questions of philanthropy with something beyond the impulses of emotion is evident, and everywhere help is being given to those heroic men and women who are devoting themselves to the practical and essentially scientific tasks. It is a good and inspiring thing to recall occasionally the heroism, for example, of the men who risked and sacrificed their lives to discover the facts about yellow fever, a sacrifice for which untold generations will bless them; and this same spirit has animated the professions of medicine and surgery.

SCIENTIFIC RESEARCH

How far may this spirit of sacrifice properly extend? A great number of scientific men every year give up everything to arrive at some helpful contribution to the sum of human knowledge, and I have sometimes thought that good people who lightly and freely criticize their actions scarcely realize just what such criticism means. It is one thing to stand on the comfortable ground of placid inaction and put forth words of cynical wisdom, and another to plunge into the work itself and through strenuous experience earn the right to express strong conclusions.

For my own part, I have stood so much as a placid onlooker that I have not had the hardihood even to suggest how people so much more experienced and wiser in those things than I should work out the details even of those plans with which I have had the honor to be associated.

There has been a good deal of criticism, no doubt sincere, of experiments on living dumb animals, and the person who stands for the defenseless animal has such an overwhelming appeal to the emotions that it is perhaps useless to allude to the other side of the controversy. Dr. Simon Flexner, of the Institute for Medical Research, has had to face exaggerated and even sensational reports, which have no basis of truth whatever. But consider for a moment what has been accomplished recently, under the direction of Dr. Flexner in discovering a remedy for epidemic Cerebro-spinal meningitis. It is true that in discovering this cure the lives of perhaps fifteen animals were sacrificed, as I learn, most of them monkeys; but for each one of these animals which lost its life, already scores of human lives have been saved. Large-hearted men like Dr. Flexner and his associates do not permit unnecessary pain to defenseless animals.

I have been deeply interested in the story of a desperate experiment to save a child's life, told in a letter written by one of my associates soon after the event described; and it seems worthy of repeating. Dr. Alexis Carrel has been associated with Dr. Flexner and his work, and his wonderful skill has been the result of his experiments and experiences.

A WONDERFUL SURGICAL OPERATION

"Dr. Alexis Carrel, one of the Institute's staff, has been making some interesting studies in experimental surgery, and has successfully transplanted organs from one animal to another, and blood vessels from one species to another. He had the opportunity recently of applying the skill thus acquired to the saving of a human life under circumstances which attracted great interest among the medical fraternity of this city. One of the best known of the younger surgeons in New York had a child born early last March, which developed a disease in which the blood, for some reason, exudes from the blood vessels into the tissues of the body, and ordinarily the child dies of this internal hemorrhage. When this child was five days old it was evident that it was dying. The father and his brother, who is one of the most distinguished men in the profession, and one or two other doctors were in consultation with reference to it, but considered the case entirely hopeless.

"It so happened that the father had been impressed with the work which Dr. Carrel had been doing at the Institute, and had spent several days with him studying his methods. He became convinced that the only possibility of saving the child's life was by the direct transfusion of blood. While this has been done between adults, the blood vessels of a young infant are so delicate that it seemed impossible that the operation could be successfully carried on. It is necessary not only that the blood vessels of the two persons should be united together, but it must be done in such a way that the interior lining of the vessels, which is a smooth, shiny tissue, should be continuous. If the blood comes in contact with the muscular coat of the blood vessels, it will clot and stop the circulation.

"Fortunately, Dr. Carrel had been experimenting on the blood vessels of some very young animals, and the father was convinced that if any man in the country could perform the operation successfully, it would be he.

"It was then the middle of the night. But Dr. Carrel was called on, and when the situation was explained to him, and it was made clear that the child would die anyhow, he readily consented to attempt the operation, although expressing very slight hope of its successful outcome.

"The father offered himself as the person whose blood should be furnished to the child. It was impossible to give anesthetics to either of them. In a child of that age there is only one vein large enough to be used, and that is in the back of the leg, and deep seated. A prominent surgeon who was present exposed this vein. He said afterward that there was no sign of life in the child, and expressed the belief that the child had been, to all intents and purposes, dead for ten minutes. In view of its condition he raised the question whether it was worth while to proceed further with the attempt. The father, however, insisted upon going on, and the surgeon then exposed the radial artery in the surgeon's wrist, and was obliged to dissect it back about six inches, in order to pull it out far enough to make the connection with the child's vein.

"This part of the work the surgeon who did it afterward described as the 'blacksmith part of the job.' He said that the child's vein was about the size of a match and the consistency of wet cigarette paper, and it seemed utterly impossible for anyone to successfully unite these two vessels. Dr. Carrel, however, accomplished this feat. And then occurred what the doctors who were present described as one of the most dramatic incidents in the history of surgery. The blood from the father's artery was released, and began to flow into the child's body, amounting to about a pint. The first sign of life was a little pink tinge at the top of one of the ears, then the lips, which had become perfectly blue, began to change to red, and then suddenly, as though the child had been taken from a hot mustard bath, a pink glow broke out all over its body, and it began to cry lustily. After about eight minutes the two were separated. The child at that time was crying for food. It was fed, and from that moment began to eat and sleep regularly, and made a complete recovery.

"The father appeared before a legislative committee at Albany, in opposition to certain bills which were pending at the last session to restrict animal experimentation, and told this incident, and said at the close that when he saw Dr. Carrel's experiments he had no idea that they would so soon be available for saving human life; much less did he imagine that the life to be saved would be that of his own child."

THE FUNDAMENTAL THING IN ALL HELP

If the people can be educated to help themselves, we strike at the root of many of the evils of the world. This is the fundamental thing, and it is worth saying even if it has been said so often that its truth is lost sight of in its constant repetition.

The only thing which is of lasting benefit to a man is that which he does for himself. Money which comes to him without effort on his part is seldom a benefit and often a curse. That is the principal objection to speculation—it is not because more lose than gain, though that is true—but it is because those who gain are apt to receive more injury from their success than they would have received from failure. And so with regard to money or other things which are given by one person to another. It is only in the exceptional case that the receiver is really benefited. But, if we can help people to help themselves, then there is a permanent blessing conferred.

Men who are studying the problem of disease tell us that it is becoming more and more evident that the forces which conquer sickness are within the body itself, and that it is only when these are reduced below the normal that disease can get a foothold. The way to ward off disease, therefore, is to tone up the body generally; and, when disease has secured a foothold, the way to combat it is to help these natural resisting agencies which are in the body already. In the same way the failures which a man makes in his life are due almost always to some defect in his personality, some weakness of body, or mind, or character, will, or temperament. The only way to overcome these failings is to build up his personality from within, so that he, by virtue of what is within him, may overcome the weakness which was the cause of the failure. It is only those efforts the man himself puts forth that can really help him.

We all desire to see the widest possible distribution of the blessings of life. Many crude plans have been suggested, some of which utterly ignore the essential facts of human nature, and if carried out would perhaps drag our whole civilization down into hopeless misery. It is my belief that the principal cause for the economic differences between people is their difference in personality, and that it is only as we can assist in the wider distribution of those qualities which go to make up a strong personality that we can assist in the wider distribution of wealth. Under normal conditions the man who is strong in body, in mind, in character, and in will need never suffer want. But these qualities can never be developed in a man unless by his own efforts, and the most that any other can do for him is, as I have said, to help him to help himself.

We must always remember that there is not enough money for the work of human uplift and that there never can be. How vitally important it is, therefore, that the expenditure should go as far as possible and be used with the greatest intelligence!

I have been frank to say that I believe in the spirit of combination and cooperation when properly and fairly conducted in the world of commercial affairs, on the principle that it helps to reduce waste; and waste is a dissipation of power. I sincerely hope and thoroughly believe that this same principle will eventually prevail in the art of giving as it does in business. It is not merely the tendency of the times developed by more exacting conditions in industry, but it should make its most effective appeal to the hearts of the people who are striving to do the most good to the largest number.

SOME UNDERLYING PRINCIPLES

At the risk of making this chapter very dull, and I am told that this is a fault which inexperienced authors should avoid at all hazards, I may perhaps be pardoned if I set down here some of the fundamental principles which have been at the bottom of all my own plans. I have undertaken no work of any importance for many years which, in a general way, has not followed out these broad lines, and I believe no really constructive effort can be made in philanthropic work without such a well-defined and consecutive purpose.

My own conversion to the feeling that an organized plan was an absolute necessity came about in this way.

About the year 1890 I was still following the haphazard fashion of giving here and there as appeals presented themselves. I investigated as I could, and worked myself almost to a nervous break-down in groping my way, without sufficient guide or chart, through this ever-widening field of philanthropic endeavour. There was then forced upon me the necessity to organize and plan this department of our daily tasks on as distinct lines of progress as we did our business affairs; and I will try to describe the underlying principles we arrived at, and have since followed out, and hope still greatly to extend.

It may be beyond the pale of good taste to speak at all of such a personal subject—I am not unmindful of this—but I can make these observations with at least a little better grace because so much of the hard work and hard thinking are done by my family and associates, who devote their lives to it.

Every right-minded man has a philosophy of life, whether he knows it or not. Hidden away in his mind are certain governing principles, whether he formulates them in words or not, which govern his life. Surely his ideal ought to be to contribute all that he can, however little it may be, whether of money or service, to human progress.

Certainly one's ideal should be to use one's means, both in one's investments and in benefactions, for the advancement of civilization. But the question as to what civilization is and what are the great laws which govern its advance have been seriously studied. Our investments not less than gifts have been directed to such ends as we have thought would tend to produce these results. If you were to go into our office, and ask our committee on benevolence or our committee on investment in what they consider civilization to consist, they would say that they have found in their study that the most convenient analysis of the elements which go to make up civilization runs about as follows:

1st. Progress in the means of subsistence, that is to say, progress in abundance and variety of food-supply, clothing, shelter, sanitation, public health, commerce, manufacture, the growth of the public wealth, etc.

2nd. Progress in government and law, that is to say, in the enactment of laws securing justice and equity to every man, consistent with the largest individual liberty, and the due and orderly enforcement of the same upon all.

3rd. Progress in literature and language.

4th. Progress in science and philosophy.

5th. Progress in art and refinement.

6th. Progress in morality and religion.

If you were to ask them, as indeed they are very often asked, which of these they regard as fundamental, they would reply that they would not attempt to answer, that the question is purely an academic one, that all these go hand in hand, but that historically the first of them—namely, progress in means of subsistence—had generally preceded progress in government, in literature, in knowledge, in refinement, and in religion. Though not itself of the highest importance, it is the foundation upon which the whole superstructure of civilization is built, and without which it could not exist.

Accordingly, we have sought, so far as we could, to make investments in such a way as will tend to multiply, to cheapen, and to diffuse as universally as possible the comforts of life. We claim no credit for preferring these lines of investment. We make no sacrifices. These are the lines of largest and surest return. In this particular, namely, in cheapness, ease of acquirement, and universality of means of subsistence, our country easily surpasses that of any other in the world, though we are behind other countries, perhaps, in most of the others.

It may be asked: How is it consistent with the universal diffusion of these blessings that vast sums of money should be in single hands? The reply is, as I see it, that, while men of wealth control great sums of money, they do not and cannot use them for themselves. They have, indeed, the legal title to large properties, and they do control the investment of them, but that is as far as their own relation to them extends or can extend. The money is universally diffused, in the sense that it is kept invested, and it passes into the pay-envelope week by week.

Up to the present time no scheme has yet presented itself which seems to afford a better method of handling capital than that of individual ownership. We might put our money into the Treasury of the Nation and of the various states, but we do not find any promise in the National or state legislatures, viewed from the experiences of the past, that the funds would be expended for the general weal more effectively than under the present methods, nor do we find in any of the schemes of socialism a promise that wealth would be more wisely administered for the general good. It is the duty of men of means to maintain the title to their property and to administer their funds until some man, or body of men, shall rise up capable of administering for the general good the capital of the country better than they can.

The next four elements of progress mentioned in the enumeration above, namely, progress in government and law, in language and literature, in science and philosophy, in art and refinement, we for ourselves have thought to be best promoted by means of the higher education, and accordingly we have had the great satisfaction of putting such sums as we could into various forms of education in our own and in foreign lands—and education not merely along the lines of disseminating more generally the known, but quite as much, and perhaps even more, in promoting original investigation. An individual institution of learning can have only a narrow sphere. It can reach only a limited number of people. But every new fact discovered, every widening of the boundaries of human knowledge by research, becomes universally known to all institutions of learning, and becomes a benefaction at once to the whole race.

Quite as interesting as any phase of the work have been the new lines entered upon by our committee. We have not been satisfied with giving to causes which have appealed to us. We have felt that the mere fact that this or the other cause makes its appeal is no reason why we should give to it any more than to a thousand other causes, perhaps more worthy, which do not happen to have come under our eye. The mere fact of a personal appeal creates no claim which did not exist before, and no preference over other causes more worthy which may not have made their appeal. So this little committee of ours has not been content to let the benevolences drift into the channels of mere convenience—to give to the institutions which have sought aid and to neglect others. This department has studied the field of human progress, and sought to contribute to each of those elements which we believe tend most to promote it. Where it has not found organizations ready to its hand for such purpose, the members of the committee have sought to create them. We are still working on new, and, I hope, expanding lines, which make large demands on one's intelligence and study.

The so-called betterment work which has always been to me a source of great interest had a great influence on my life, and I refer to it here because I wish to urge in this connection the great importance of a father's keeping in close touch with his children, taking into his confidence the girls as well as the boys, who in this way learn by seeing and doing, and have their part in the family responsibilities. As my father taught me, so I have tried to teach my children. For years it was our custom to read at the table the letters we received affecting the various benevolences with which we had to do, studying the requests made for worthy purposes, and following the history and reports of institutions and philanthropic cases in which we were interested.

CHAPTER VII

The Benevolent Trust—the Value of the Coöperative Principle in Giving

Going a step farther in the plan of making benefactions increasingly effective which I took up in the last chapter under the title of "The Difficult Art of Giving," I am tempted to take the opportunity to dwell a little upon the subject of combination in charitable work, which has been something of a hobby with me for many years.

If a combination to do business is effective in saving waste and in getting better results, why is not combination far more important in philanthropic work? The general idea of cooperation in giving for education, I have felt, scored a real step in advance when Mr. Andrew Carnegie consented to become a member of the General Education Board. For in accepting a position in this directorate he has, it seems to me, stamped with his approval this vital principle of cooperation in aiding the educational institutions of our country.

I rejoice, as everybody must, in Mr. Carnegie's enthusiasm for using his wealth for the benefit of his less fortunate fellows and I think his devotion to his adopted land's welfare has set a striking example for all time.

The General Education Board, of which Mr. Carnegie has now become a member, is interesting as an example of an organization formed for the purpose of working out, in an orderly and rather scientific way, the problem of helping to stimulate and improve education in all parts of our country. What this organization may eventually accomplish, of course, no one can tell, but surely, under its present board of directors, it will go very far. Here, again, I feel that I may speak frankly and express my personal faith in its success, since I am not a member of the board, and have never attended a meeting, and the work is all done by others.

There are some other and larger plans thought out on careful and broad lines, which I have been studying for many years, and we can see that they are growing into definite shape. It is good to know that there are always unselfish men, of the best calibre, to help in every large philanthropic enterprise. One of the most satisfactory and stimulating pieces of good fortune that has come to me is the evidence that so many busy people are willing to turn aside from their work in pressing fields of labor and to give their best thoughts and energies without compensation to the work of human uplift. Doctors, clergymen, lawyers, as well as many high-grade men of affairs, are devoting their best and most unselfish efforts to some of the plans that we are all trying to work out.

Take, as one example of many similar cases, Mr. Robert C. Ogden, who for years, while devoting himself to an exacting business, still found time, supported by wonderful enthusiasm, to give force by his own personality to work done in difficult parts of the educational world, particularly to improving the common school system of the South. His efforts have been wisely directed along fundamental lines which must produce results through the years to come.

Fortunately my children have been as earnest as I, and much more diligent, in carefully and intelligently carrying out the work already begun, and agree with me that at least the same energy and thought should be expended in the proper and effective use of money when acquired as was exerted in the earning of it.

The General Education Board has made, or is making, a careful study of the location, aims, work, resources, administration, and educational value, present and prospective, of the institutions of higher learning in the United States. The board makes its contributions, averaging something like two million dollars a year, on the most careful comparative study of needs and opportunities throughout the country. Its records are open to all. Many benefactors of education are availing themselves of these disinterested inquiries, and it is hoped that more will do so.

A large number of individuals are contributing to the support of educational institutions in our country. To help an inefficient, ill-located, unnecessary school is a waste. I am told by those who have given most careful study to this problem that it is highly probable that enough money has been squandered on unwise educational projects to have built up a national system of higher education adequate to our needs if the money had been properly directed to that end. Many of the good people who bestow their beneficence on education may well give more thought to investigating the character of the enterprises that they are importuned to help, and this study ought to take into account the kind of people who are responsible for their management, their location, and the facilities supplied by other institutions round about. A thorough examination such as this is generally quite impossible for an individual, and he either declines to give from lack of accurate knowledge, or he may give without due consideration. If, however, this work of inquiry is done, and well done, by the General Education Board, through officers of intelligence, skill, and sympathy, trained to the work, important and needed service is rendered. The walls of sectarian exclusiveness are fast disappearing, as they should, and the best people are standing shoulder to shoulder as they attack the great problems of general uplift.

ROMAN CATHOLIC CHARITIES

Just here it occurs to me to testify to the fact that the Roman Catholic Church, as I have observed in my experience, has advanced a long way in this direction. I have been surprised to learn how far a given sum of money has gone in the hands of priests and nuns, and how really effective is their use of it. I fully appreciate the splendid service done by other workers in the field, but I have seen the organization of the Roman Church secure better results with a given sum of money than other Church organizations are accustomed to secure from the same expenditure. I speak of this merely to point the value of the principle of organization, in which I believe so heartily. It is unnecessary to dwell upon the centuries of experience which the Church of Rome has gone through to perfect a great power of organization.

Studying these problems has been a source of the greatest interest to me. My assistants, quite distinct from any board, have an organization of sufficient size to investigate the many requests that come to us. This is done from the office of our committee in New York. For an individual to attempt to keep any close watch of single cases would be impossible. I am called upon to explain this fact many times. To read the hundreds of letters daily received at our office would be beyond the power of any one man, and surely, if the many good people who write would only reflect a little, they must realize that it is impossible for me personally to consider their applications.

The plan that we have worked out, and I hope improved upon year after year, has been the result of experience, and I refer to it now only as one contribution to a general subject which is of such great moment to earnest people; and this must be my excuse for speaking so frankly.

THE APPEALS THAT COME

The reading, assorting, and investigating of the hundreds of letters of appeal which are received daily at my office are attended to by a department organized for this purpose. The task is not so difficult as at first it might seem. The letters are, to be sure, of great variety, from all sorts of people in every condition of life, and indeed, from all parts of the world. Four-fifths of these letters are, however, requests for money for personal use, with no other title to consideration than that the writer would be gratified to have it.

There remain numbers of requests which all must recognize as worthy of notice. These may be divided, roughly, as follows:

The claims of local charities. The town or city in which one lives has a definite appeal to all its citizens, and all good neighbours will wish to coöperate with friends and fellow townsmen. But these local charities, hospitals, kindergartens, and the like, ought not to make appeal outside the local communities which they serve. The burden should be carried by the people who are on the spot and who are, or should be, most familiar with local needs.

Then come the national and international claims. These properly appeal especially to men of large means throughout the country, whose wealth admits of their doing something more than assist in caring for the local charities. There are many great national and international philanthropic and Christian organizations that cover the whole field of world-wide charity; and, while people of reputed wealth all receive appeals from individual workers throughout the world for personal assistance, the prudent and thoughtful giver will, more and more, choose these great and responsible organizations as the medium for his gifts and the distribution of his funds to distant fields. This has been my custom, and the experience of every day serves only to confirm its wisdom.

The great value of dealing with an organization which knows all the facts, and can best decide just where the help can be applied to the best advantage, has impressed itself upon me through the results of long years of experience. For example, one is asked to give in a certain field of missionary work a sum, for a definite purpose—let us say a hospital. To comply with this request will take, say, $10,000. It seems wise and natural to give this amount. The missionary who wants this money is working under the direction of a strong and capable religious denomination.

Suppose the request is referred to the manager of the board of this denomination, and it transpires that there are many good reasons why a new hospital is not badly needed at this point, and by a little good management the need of this missionary can be met by another hospital in its neighborhood; whereas another missionary in another place has no such possibility for any hospital facilities whatever. There is no question that the money should be spent in the place last named. These conditions the managers of all the mission stations know, although perhaps the one who is giving the money never heard of them, and in my judgment, he is wise in not acting until he has consulted these men of larger information.

It is interesting to follow the mental processes that some excellent souls go through to cloud their consciences when they consider what their duty actually is. For instance, one man says: "I do not believe in giving money to street beggars." I agree with him; I do not believe in the practice either; but that is not a reason why one should be exempt from doing something to help the situation represented by the street beggar. Because one does not yield to the importunities of such people is exactly the reason one should join and uphold the charity organization societies of one's own locality, which deal justly and humanely with this class, separating the worthy from the unworthy.

Another says: "I don't give to such and such a board, because I have read that of the money given only half or less actually gets to the person needing help." This is often not a true statement of fact, as proved again and again, and even if it were true in part it does not relieve the possible giver from the duty of helping to make the organization more efficient. By no possible chance is it a valid excuse for closing up one's pocketbook and dismissing the whole subject from one's mind.

INSTITUTIONS AS THEY RELATE TO EACH OTHER

Surely it is wise to be careful not to duplicate effort and not to inaugurate new charities in fields already covered, but rather to strengthen and perfect those already at work. There is a great deal of rivalry and a vast amount of duplication, and one of the most difficult things in giving is to ascertain when the field is fully covered. Many people simply consider whether the institution to which they are giving is thoughtfully and well managed, without stopping to discover whether the field is not already occupied by others; and for this reason one ought not to investigate a single institution by itself, but always in its relation to all similar institutions in the territory. Here is a case in point:

A number of enthusiastic people had a plan for founding an orphan asylum which was to be conducted by one of our strongest religious denominations. The raising of the necessary funds was begun, and among the people who were asked to subscribe was a man who always made it a practice to study the situation carefully before committing himself to a contribution. He asked one of the promoters of the new institution how many beds the present asylums serving this community provided, how efficient they

115

were, where located, and what particular class of institution was lacking in the community.

To none of these questions were answers forthcoming, so he had this information gathered on his own account with the purpose of helping to make the new plan effective. His studies revealed the fact that the city where the new asylum was to be built was so well provided with such institutions that there were already vastly more beds for children than there were applicants to fill them, and that the field was well and fully covered. These facts being presented to the organizers of the enterprise, it was shown that no real need for such an institution existed. I wish I might add that the scheme was abandoned. It was not. Such charities seldom are when once the sympathies of the worthy people, however misinformed, are heartily enlisted.

It may be urged that doing the work in this systematic and apparently cold-blooded way leaves out of consideration, to a large extent, the merits of individual cases. My contention is that the organization of work in combination should not and does not stifle the work of individuals, but strengthens and stimulates it. The orderly combination of philanthropic effort is growing daily, and at the same time the spirit of broad philanthropy never was so general as it is now.

THE CLAIM OF HIGHER EDUCATION

The giver who works out these problems for himself will, no doubt, find many critics. So many people see the pressing needs of every-day life that possibly they fail to realize those which are, if less obvious, of an even larger significance—for instance, the great claims of higher education. Ignorance is the source of a large part of the poverty and a vast amount of the crime in the world—hence the need of education. If we assist the highest forms of education—in whatever field—we secure the widest influence in enlarging the boundaries of human knowledge; for all the new facts discovered or set in motion become the universal heritage. I think we cannot overestimate the importance of this matter. The mere fact that most of the great achievements in science, medicine, art, and literature are the flower of the higher education is sufficient. Some great writer will one day show how these things have ministered to the wants of all the people, educated and uneducated, high and low, rich and poor, and made life more what we all wish it to be.

The best philanthropy is constantly in search of the finalities—a search for cause, an attempt to cure evils at their source. My interest in the University of Chicago has been enhanced by the fact that while it has comprehensively considered the other features of a collegiate course, it has given so much attention to research.

DR. WILLIAM R. HARPER

The mention of this promising young institution always brings to my mind the figure of Dr. William R. Harper, whose enthusiasm for its work was so great that no vision of its future seemed too large.

My first meeting with Dr. Harper was at Vassar College, where one of my daughters was a student. He used to come, as the guest of Dr. James M. Taylor, the president, to lecture on Sundays; and as I frequently spent week-ends there, I saw and talked much with the young professor, then of Yale, and caught in some degree the contagion of his enthusiasm.

When the university had been founded, and he had taken the presidency, our great ambition was to secure the best instructors and to organize the new institution, unhampered by traditions, according to the most modern ideals. He raised millions of dollars among the people of Chicago and the Middle West, and won the personal interest of their leading citizens. Here lay his great strength, for he secured not only their money but their loyal support and strong personal interest—the best kind of help and cooperation. He built even better than he knew. His lofty ideals embodied in the university awakened a deeper interest in higher education throughout the Central West, and stirred individuals, denominations, and legislatures to effective action. The world will probably never realize how largely the present splendid university system of the Central Western States is due indirectly to the genius of this man.

With all his extraordinary power of work and his executive and organizing ability, Dr. Harper was a man of exquisite personal charm. We count it among the rich and delightful experiences of our home-life that Dr. and Mrs. Harper could occasionally spend days together with us for a brief respite from the exacting cares and responsibilities of the university work. As a friend and companion, in daily intercourse, no one could be more delightful than he.

It has been my good fortune to contribute at various times to the University of Chicago, of which Dr. Harper was president, and the newspapers not unnaturally supposed at such times that he used the occasions of our personal association to secure these contributions. The cartoonists used to find this a fruitful theme. They would picture Dr. Harper as a hypnotist waving his magic spell, or would represent him forcing his way into my inner office where I was pictured as busy cutting coupons and from which delightful employment I incontinently fled out of the window at sight of him; or they would represent me as fleeing across rivers on cakes of floating ice with Dr. Harper in hot pursuit; or perhaps he would be following close on my trail, like the wolf in the Russian story, in inaccessible country retreats, while I escaped only by means of the slight delays I occasioned him by now and then dropping a million-dollar bill, which he would be obliged to stop and pick up.

These cartoons were intended to be very amusing, and some of them certainly did have a flavour of humour, but they were never humorous to Dr. Harper. They were in fact a source of deep humiliation to him, and I am sure he would, were he living, be glad to have me say, as I now do, that during the entire period of his presidency of the University of Chicago, he never once either wrote me a letter or asked me personally for a dollar of money for the University of Chicago. In the most intimate daily intercourse with him in my home, the finances of the University of Chicago were never canvassed or discussed.

The method of procedure in this case has been substantially the same as with all other contributions. The presentation of the needs of the university has been made in writing by the officers of the university, whose special duty it is to prepare its budgets and superintend its finances. A committee of the trustees, with the president, have annually conferred, at a fixed time, with our Department of Benevolence, as to its needs. Their conclusions have generally been entirely unanimous and I have found no occasion hitherto seriously to depart from their recommendations. There have been no personal interviews and no personal solicitations. It has been a pleasure to me to make these contributions, but that pleasure has arisen out of the fact that the university is located in a great centre of empire; that it has rooted itself in the affections and interest of the people among whom it is located; that it is doing a great and needed work—in fine, that it has been able to attract and to justify the contributions of its patrons East and West. It is not personal interviews and impassioned appeals, but sound and justifying worth, that should attract and secure the funds of philanthropy.

The people in great numbers who are constantly importuning me for personal interviews in behalf of favourite causes err in supposing that the interview, were it possible, is the best way, or even a good way, of securing what they want. Our practice has been uniformly to request applicants to state their cases tersely, but nevertheless as fully as they think necessary, in writing. Their application is carefully considered by very competent people chosen for this purpose. If, thereupon, personal interviews are found desirable by our assistants, they are invited from our office.

Written presentations form the necessary basis of investigation, of consultation, and comparison of views between the different members of our staff, and of the final presentation to me.

It is impossible to conduct this department of our work in any other way. The rule requiring written presentation as against the interview is enforced and adhered to not, as the applicant sometimes supposes, as a cold rebuff to him, but in order to secure for his cause, if it be a good one, the careful consideration which is its due—a consideration that cannot be given in a mere verbal interview.

THE REASON FOR CONDITIONAL GIFTS

It is easy to do harm in giving money. To give to institutions which should be supported by others is not the best philanthropy. Such giving only serves to dry up the natural springs of charity.

It is highly important that every charitable institution shall have at all times the largest possible number of current contributors. This means that the institution shall constantly be making its appeals; but, if these constant appeals are to be successful, the institution is forced to do excellent work and meet real and manifest needs. Moreover, the interest of many people affords the best assurance of wise economy and unselfish management as well as of continued support.

We frequently make our gifts conditional on the giving of others, not because we wish to force people to do their duty, but because we wish in this way to root the institution in the affections of as many people as possible who, as contributors, become personally concerned, and thereafter may be counted on to give to the institution their watchful interest and cooperation. Conditional gifts are often criticized, and sometimes, it may be, by people who have not thought the matter out fully.

Criticism which is deliberate, sober, and fair is always valuable and it should be welcomed by all who desire progress. I have had at least my full share of adverse criticism, but I can truly say that it has not embittered me, nor left me with any harsh feeling against a living soul. Nor do I wish to be critical of those whose conscientious judgment, frankly expressed, differs from my own. No matter how noisy the pessimists may be, we know that the world is getting better steadily and rapidly, and that is a good thing to remember in our moments of depression or humiliation.

THE BENEVOLENT TRUSTS

To return to the subject of the Benevolent Trusts, which is a name for corporations to manage the business side of benefactions. The idea needs, and to be successful must have, the help of men who have been trained along practical lines. The best men of business should be attracted by its possibilities for good. When it is eventually worked out, as it will be in some form, and probably in a better one than we can now forecast, how worthy it will be of the efforts of our ablest men!

We shall have the best charities supported generously and adequately, managed with scientific efficiency by the ablest men, who will gladly he held strictly accountable to the donors of the money, not only for the correct financing of the funds, but for the intelligent and effective use of every penny. To-day the whole machinery of benevolence is conducted upon more or less haphazard principles. Good men and women are wearing out their lives to raise money to sustain institutions which are conducted by more less or unskilled methods. This is a tremendous waste of our best material.

We cannot afford to have great souls who are capable of doing the most effective work slaving to raise the money. That should be a business man's task, and he should be supreme in managing the machinery of the expenses. The teachers, the workers, and the inspired leaders of the people should be relieved of these pressing and belittling money cares. They have more than enough to do in tilling their tremendous and never fully occupied field, and they should be free from any care which might in any wise divert them from that work.

When these Benevolent Trusts come into active being, such organizations on broad lines will be sure to attract the brains of the best men we have in our commercial affairs, as great business opportunities attract them now. Our successful business men as a class, and the exceptions only prove the truth of the assertion, have a high standard of. I have sometimes been tempted to say that our clergymen could gain by knowing the essentials of business life better. The closer association with men of affairs would, I think, benefit both classes. People who have had much to do with ministers and those who hold confidential positions in our churches have at times had surprising experiences in meeting what is sometimes practiced in the way of ecclesiastical business, because these good men have had so little of business training in the work-a-day world.

The whole system of proper relations, whether it be in commerce, or in the Church, or in the sciences, rests on honor. Able business men seek to confine their dealings to people who tell the truth and keep their promises; and the representatives of the Church, who are often prone to attack business men as a type of what is selfish and mean, have some great lessons to learn, and they will gladly learn them as these two types of workers grow closer together.

The Benevolent Trusts, when they come, will raise these standards; they will look the facts in the face; they will applaud and sustain the effective workers and institutions; and they will uplift the intelligent standard of good work in helping all the people chiefly to help themselves. There are already signs that these combinations are coming, and coming quickly, and in the directorates of these trusts you will eventually find the flower of our American manhood, the men who not only know how to make money, but who accept the great responsibility of administering it wisely.

A few years ago, on the occasion of the decennial anniversary of the University of Chicago, I was attending a university dinner, and having been asked to speak I had jotted down a few notes.

When the time arrived to stand up and face these guests—men of worth and position—my notes meant nothing to me. As I thought of the latent power of good that rested with these rich and influential people I was greatly affected. I threw down my notes and started to plead for my Benevolent Trust plan.

"You men," I said, "are always looking forward to do something for good causes. I know how very busy you are. You work in a treadmill from which you see no escape. I can easily understand that you feel that it is beyond your present power carefully to study the needs of humanity, and that you wait to give until you have considered many things and decided upon some course of action. Now, why not do with what you can give to others as you do with what you want to keep for yourself and your children: Put it into a Trust? You would not place a fortune for your children in the hands of an inexperienced person, no matter how good he might be. Let us be as careful with the money we would spend for the benefit of others as if we were laying it aside for our own family's future use. Directors carry on these affairs in your behalf. Let us erect a foundation, a Trust, and engage directors who will make it a life work to manage, with our personal cooperation, this business of benevolence properly and effectively. And I beg of you, attend to it *now*, don't wait."

I confess I felt most strongly on the subject, and I feel so now.

www.ingramcontent.com/pod-product-compliance
Lightning Source LLC
Chambersburg PA
CBHW030639150426
42813CB00050B/153